D0171798

THE HANDBOOK OF
STYLE

THE HANDBOOK OF
STYLE

Expert Fashion and Beauty Advice

As told to Francine Maroukian and Sarah Woodruff

QUIRK BOOKS
PHILADELPHIA

Copyright © 2007 by Francine Maroukian

All rights reserved. No part of this book may be reproduced in any form without written permission from the publisher.

Library of Congress Cataloging in Publication Number: 2006928221
ISBN-10: 1-59474-053-4
ISBN-13: 978-1-59474-053-4

Printed in China
Typeset in Conduit ITC, Octavian MT, and Weiss

Designed by Karen Onorato
Illustrations by Jesse Ewing
Production management by Stephanie O'Neill McKenna

Distributed in North America by Chronicle Books
85 Second Street
San Francisco, CA 94105

10 9 8 7 6 5 4 3 2 1

Quirk Books
215 Church Street
Philadelphia, PA 19106
www.quirkbooks.com

CONTENTS

INTRODUCTION

We are the sort of people who like to ask for and give advice; we've also been known to rip how-to pages out of style magazines and save them. Put these two things together and you get friends who give each other fashion and beauty advice based on what they read. But it doesn't always work as well as we'd like.

Many of the articles we've stashed away only tell us what to buy, not what to do. Sure, we'd go out and track down everything we were told to buy, but then what? We wanted more information, and for that, we needed experts. We also needed some efficient way to record and store their advice. It might seem obvious, but we felt like geniuses the day we realized that we could throw away our messy folders of old magazine articles and make our own book.

Our first decision was easy: Style—especially the classic but modern style that we aspire to in our own lives—must include beauty and fashion advice (unlike most of the other "expert" books that focus on one or the other), and we went after people whose expertise makes them leaders in those fields. Of course, when we got out there and began to interview the specialists who could answer our questions, we discovered something important: Style advice is hard, primarily because it is so fluid. We were lucky to connect to style leaders like Evelyn Lauder, a longtime creative force for Estée Lauder, and Hanky Panky's President and Creative Director Gale Epstein, whose designs are included in the Metropolitan Museum of Art's permanent costume exhibit and who practically invented the thong, so our experts had a lot of advice to offer. We then pared down their information into what we envisioned from the day we started: an instructional step-by-step design—a recipe for style.

Like doctors who won't prescribe over the phone, our experts didn't want to generalize away the usefulness of their information. (Face it, when you truly aspire to style, there is no "one size fits all," and that applies to advice as well.) That's why when you're on a quest for a bathing suit or a pair of jeans that fit and flatter, or when you're looking for a shade of red lipstick that works for your particular skin tone, you need a combination of good shopping genes, perseverance, and just plain luck. The only advice every expert agreed on is this: When you find the right stuff, buy in multiples.

But for quintessential fashion classics—like buying a pearl necklace, getting the haircut you really want, or figuring out the intricacies of lip gloss—you can count on our experts (who represent some of the most prestigious beauty and fashion companies in the world) to give you advice that goes beyond their brand.

Paula Dorf, who started as a film and runway makeup artist before opening her eponymous cosmetics company, didn't just tell us how to use makeup brushes—she taught us about brush construction right down to the tuft and why differently shaped bristles produce different results. From Donald J Pliner, who brought great European designers like Stephan Kelian into the country before launching his own line, we learned what design details to look for if we want to wear comfortable but sexy shoes—an admirable goal that can actually be achieved. And Rafe Totengco, who won the ACE Award for Best Accessories Designer, deconstructed the shapes and features of the five must-have hand-bags. It added up to an education for us, and we hope for you as well.

Use our experts' advice to give yourself a style upgrade, or better yet, do what we do: Tell a friend.

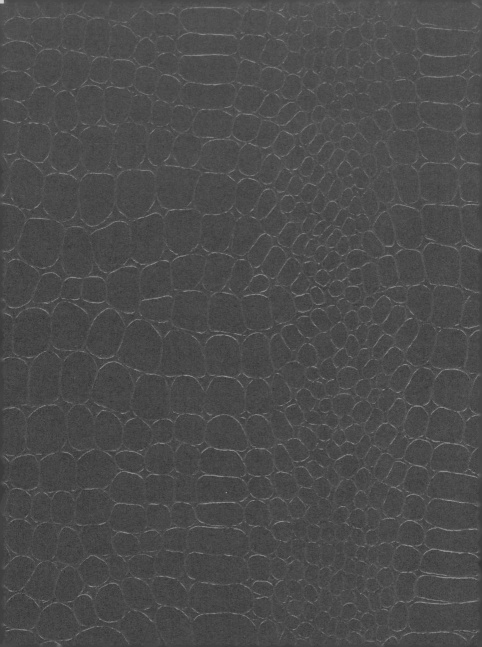

How to Get the Haircut You Want

by Paul Labrecque of Paul Labrecque Salon & Spa

Trained in the art of haircutting and coloring in London, industry visionary Paul Labrecque's revolutionary treatments (thermal reconditioning, color varnishing) and progressive hair-styling techniques have spawned two successful Manhattan salon/spas, as well as an award-winning line of signature hair-care products. Paul Labrecque Salon & Spa is a consistent New York magazine "best of" and hosts a long list of well-known clients, from Natasha Richardson and Kevin Spacey to Sting and Trudie Styler.

To get a good haircut you must be aware of your hair's natural texture. Whether it's wavy, curly, or straight, don't fight it. I encourage all my clients to work with their hair's natural beauty, and the result is a haircut that never looks forced and is simple to maintain while still looking sexy and sophisticated.

STEP 1: Consult your stylist. Bear in mind that we are visually oriented people, so come in with ideas and pictures of the style you want. These should be used as an inspiration, not an exact blueprint, of course: The hairstyle you want will have to be adapted to suit your hair's individual characteristics. I always encourage my clients to keep an open mind and listen to my recommendations, as it is my business to understand the cutting techniques and how hair moves, but I also take into account my clients' lifestyle, work environment, personality, and how much time they are willing to spend on maintenance each day. The idea is to develop the kind of relationship in which your stylist can tell you what will not work, even if you are insistent.

A Cut for Every Shape

The shape of your face will determine your most flattering cut:

Round-shaped faces need height and not width on the sides.

Pear-shaped faces need width on the sides and wispiness in the cheek area.

Square-shaped faces need softness, like a side part—nothing geometric like blunt bangs.

Heart-shaped faces look best with jaw-length hair in one solid length.

Oval-shaped faces can wear almost any style, although a cut that is slightly fuller on the sides is most flattering.

STEP 2: Reach an agreement with your stylist so there are no surprises. Even when you have worked with the same person for years, there must be enough communication between you that you can replicate the finished look of the hair at home. Ask what your stylist is planning. If you don't agree, say so. The consultation is intended to discover if you and the stylist will be able to achieve the cut that is right for you—if you can't reach an agreement, you may have to choose another stylist.

STEP 3: Cooperate with your stylist so he or she can give you the most accurate cut. Wear the salon smock so your stylist can cut close to the skin. Never wear your glasses, as they can hold your hair back, and sit straight in the chair, legs uncrossed. (Crossing your legs throws off your body's balance and can give you a lopsided look when the stylist cuts the initial line.) Be prepared to stand so that your stylist can determine the right length for the base line of your cut.

STEP 4: Study your finished haircut. Your stylist will offer you a large hand mirror so you can examine your hair from all angles. Talk about what you like and don't like. Your stylist should not be anxious or upset if you ask for an adjustment. Believe me, we would much rather hear your complaints then and there, when we can do something about it.

STEP 5: Ask your stylist for advice on your hair's cleansing and conditioning needs. Give your hair the same attention you give your skin. Maintenance should be simple. If you cannot maintain your cut at home, you will never be happy with the result.

⚠ **"I hate my haircut!"** If you get a cut you don't like from your regular stylist, remember—it's just one day in your relationship, and he or she deserves another chance. If it's the first time you have seen this particular stylist, perhaps your consultation went wrong. Or perhaps the cut became unmanageable when you tried to replicate the style at home. Make an appointment to discuss what went wrong. Sometimes the only way to deal with a bad cut is to let it grow: Cutting it again might make it worse. Ask the stylist to make adjustments that help blend the poorly styled pieces into the rest of your hair.

FM: Define "trendy."

PL: I don't think "trendy" is necessarily a negative word or has to mean "for the moment." Trendy, fashion-forward cuts are looks for people who know their personal style and are confident about wearing it. You can always recognize someone who is comfortable in their own skin.

FM: Who is your favorite style icon?

PL: Yves Saint Laurent: Timeless. Classic. Sexy.

FM: What is your favorite fashion scene from a movie?

PL: Barbra Streisand in *Funny Girl*, when she is standing on stage dressed in leopard skin and singing "My Man."

EXTRA HELP

Keep Talking

Talking to your stylist while he or she is cutting your hair is part of the salon experience. Newer stylists may talk less because they need to concentrate more, but those of us who have been cutting hair for a long time have relationships with our clients. We see you on a regular basis, and continual communication remains the best guarantee that you will always get the haircut you want. With every change the body makes, the shape of the face changes, and your hair has to change with it. We are there to help you with your metamorphosis.

HOW TO TRIM YOUR BANGS

by Kevin Woon of Woon Salon

At seventeen, Malaysian-born Kevin Woon moved to New York City and supplemented his college tuition with a job as a hairstylist's assistant. Woon then trained at Oribe's Fifth Avenue salon and eventually assisted on fashion shows for designers such as Dolce & Gabbana, Valentino, and Prada. He is now the proprietor of his own Manhattan salon, and his hairstyles can be seen in the most highly regarded fashion magazines, from Harper's Bazaar *to* Vogue.

To me, all bangs are sexy: long and blunt, almost covering the eyes, looking mysterious like a rocker chick, like Chrissie Hynde wears; Deborah Harry's Blondie choppy fringe, so overgrown she really couldn't see much but she looked great anyway; even a refined, sophisticated side-swept style. In a way, bangs represent youth—they bring back that "school girl" look and make women feel younger.

Bang maintenance might require a different schedule than the rest of your haircut. The best solution is to establish the kind of relationship with your stylist in which bang trims are just a part of the program. However, if you find yourself in need of a bang trim and cannot get to your stylist, you may have to do it yourself. But don't make a habit of it—bangs are not separate from your overall hairstyle and should be handled professionally.

STEP 1: Find the right equipment. You need a lit-from-above mirror that you can stand in front of (don't sit down) as well as pointy-tipped scissors with balanced finger rings like those your stylist uses. You can buy a less expensive pair than the scissors used by your stylist, but you really must use the right kind.

STEP 2: Wash your hair, but don't put in any products. Your hair should be dry and product free so you are working with its natural texture. Arrange your bangs naturally—the way you usually wear them—and don't hold or flatten them into place.

STEP 3: Hold the scissors pointing up toward the ceiling at about a 30-degree angle. If the ceiling is at 12:00, the scissors should be pointing at 11:00. Following their natural shape, start cutting into your bangs vertically with tiny, tiny snips. Be extremely cautious.

STEP 4: Use your hand to ruffle your bangs, shaking the tiny hairs loose and allowing the bangs to fall in shape naturally. Repeat step 3 (cautiously) if you need to cut more.

⚠ **"I cut my bangs too short."** Mistakes happen, but there are only a few ways to rectify this problem. For those who are adventurous and willing to change, it may be time for a shorter haircut. You can also use hair accessories (hairpins or clips, simple or decorated) or products like gel and pomade to push your shorter bangs back or to the side. Whatever you decide, call your stylist immediately to set up your next appointment!

Q&A

FM: Best style tip you ever got, and from whom?
KW: Don't try too hard—completely self-generated.

FM: Who is film's most fashionable leading lady?
KW: Hong Kong actress Maggie Cheung, for her all-around great style.

FM: What is your favorite fashion scene from a movie?
KW: The entire Franc Roddam film *Quadrophenia*. I love the jackets, the shoes—the whole Mod thing.

HOW TO MANAGE NATURALLY CURLY HAIR

by Lorraine Massey of Devachan Hair and Departure Lounge

At thirteen, Lorraine Massey started her haircutting career in a local salon in Leicester, England. She later studied with Martin Smith, the artistic director of Remi-Toni & Guy. After travels to Hong Kong, Japan, and the Philippines, she teamed with Denis DaSilva to open Devachan, a full-service spa in Lower Manhattan. Passionate about caring for curly hair, Massey is the author of the how-to manifesto Curly Girl *and cocreator of the DevaCurl hair care line.*

Curls were the bane of my existence from the first moment I could look into a mirror. When asked what I wanted for my third birthday, I requested a long, black, straight wig. But that bane is now my passion. Accepting that this little garden atop my head comes with me wherever I go, I've come to love my curly hair. Curls go in and out of style because most people don't understand "curl needs"—they just try to make them go away. Once you are smart enough to realize that you can't fight Mother Nature, you can make peace with your hair and become an advanced curly girl—one who understands, accepts, and has mastery of her curls. Here are four steps to freedom.

STEP 1: Apply hair cleanser to your thoroughly wet hair. Use your fingertips to apply a sodium lauryl sulphate–free hair cleanser directly to the scalp, massaging to break up any dirt residue or build-up. Rinse with water.

STEP 2: Generously distribute an emollient-rich conditioner throughout the hair. Gently comb through, using only your fingers. Pry out any tangles. If hair is severely dehydrated, leave in all the conditioner; if you have a finer curl that weighs down easily, leave in a small amount, rinsing the rest away.

The Curl Commandments

If you think of your hair as a priceless heavenly fabric that needs life-aids instead of band-aids, you will soon be sporting terminally healthy hair!

1. **Never use alcohol-based petrifying gel;** it actually contributes to the frizz factor. Always choose a clear, plastic- and resin-free gel as directed above; it will remain in the hair 24 hours a day, protecting and providing the critical moisture curly hair needs.

2. **Resist the temptation to use a blow fryer.** Let hair dry naturally or, if you must, use a blow fryer that has a diffuser. Curls do very well with dry heat as long as it is not blown directly or harshly on the hair.

3. **Never touch hair while it is drying.** As long as you are not touching your hair, you are not creating friction. Friction causes frizz—a curl begging for moisture, definition, and direction.

4. **For more body, use your fingers to loosen curls from underneath,** never from the surface where curls are most vulnerable.

5. **Never use a brush or comb.**

STEP 3: Squeeze out excess water and conditioner. Tilt your head and, holding paper towels or an old T-shirt (these create less friction and so reduce frizz) with both hands, "scrunch" your hair, moving upward from the bottom of your hair to the top to squeeze out excess water and conditioner.

STEP 4: Apply hair gel. Evenly distribute a palmful of clear, plastic- and resin-free gel into both hands (the actual amount depends on the length of your hair), bend over, and "scrunch" your hair from the bottom up. Gently bring your head up, shake out gently, and allow curls to fall naturally.

Q&A

FM: What's the worst fashion faux pas?
LM: Letting your hair wear you.

FM: Define "fashion forward."
LM: You wearing your hair.

FM: Who is film's most fashionable leading lady?
LM: Eddie Izzard.

How to Bond with Your Blow Dryer

by Hiro Haraguchi of Hiro Haraguchi Hair Salon

A native of Japan, Hiro Haraguchi began his New York training at the fashionable Suga Salon, where he met his mentor, designer Vera Wang, and became her personal stylist. After working in Oribe and Garren salons, as well as styling for Marc Jacobs and Anna Sui fashion shows, Haraguchi opened his own salon in September 2002. His goal is to be a doctor for the hair, offering individualized consultation, cut, styling, and aftercare.

There is no one way to blow out your hair, just as there is no one haircut. However, a powerful professional dryer with at least 2,000 watts and a directional nozzle to concentrate the air flow is essential for proper styling.

Crumple an empty plastic shopping bag in the palm of your hand. When you blow lightly across it, none of the folds in the bag move. But if you blow strongly and directly, the ripples in the bag lay down flat. The same is true of your hair. If your dryer isn't strong enough, the hair cuticle won't lay down flat. It will curl up, and your hair will be frizzy. The flat cuticle is also what makes your hair shiny. The kind of brush you select and the amount of tension you apply to the hair while drying also contribute to the effectiveness of your blow out.

Here are my solutions for the four most widespread problems my clients encounter.

PROBLEM: FINE HAIR; WANTS VOLUME.

STEP 1: After shampooing, section your hair into portions about the width of the brush. Holding a section away from your head (like a ray of the sun), brush both sides of the hair from roots to ends so that all the hairs are going in the same direction.

STEP 2: Use a round, natural bristle brush to roll the hair from the ends to the roots. Your brush barrel should be large enough so the hair wraps around it only one and a half times. There should be tension as you roll and a snug fit at the root end to help make your hair stand up at the roots and produce volume. Holding the hair taut against the brush as you roll also allows the hair to sink down into and be held by the bristles (instead of just lying on top of the curve of the brush).

STEP 3: Using the directional nozzle, dry the rolled hair on both sides of the brush. Do not remove the brush while the hair is hot. Let the hair cool around the shape of the brush for 10 to 15 seconds. Do not remove the brush by pulling it through the hair. Wiggle the brush slightly, and gently remove it as you wrap the curled hair around your finger and lay it in place.

STEP 4: Once hair is completely dry, seal it with a finishing product. Apply gloss or spray and tousle hair with your fingers or brush it into place.

BEST CUT: Avoid one-length hair; volume will be boosted by moderate layering.

PROBLEM: FRIZZY HAIR; WANTS SHINY HAIR.

STEP 1: After shampooing, section your hair as directed in step 1 on page 23; if your hair is very frizzy, your sections can be smaller than the width of the brush. Holding a section away from your head, brush both sides of the hair from roots to ends so that all the hairs are going in the same direction.

STEP 2: Using a round natural-bristle brush as directed in step 2 above, angle the brush in toward your head and place it as close to the root as possible. Lay the section of hair over the crest of the brush and roll the handle slightly until the hair sinks down into and is held taut by the bristles.

STEP 3: Placing the directional nozzle at the top of the brush, roll your wrist, pulling the brush through your hair. Follow the path from the root to the ends with the dryer. The hair doesn't have to be pulled so tight that it hurts your scalp, but tension is required to roll the hair cuticle under, which will prevent frizz and bestow shine.

BEST CUT: Choose a layered hairstyle.

PROBLEM: HAIR IS TOO HEAVY AND STRAIGHT; WANTS BODY.

STEP 1: After shampooing, comb your hair with a wide-tooth comb.

STEP 2: Dry your hair about 80 percent dry. Use the directional nozzle and hold the dryer about one inch (2.5 cm) away from your hair. Alternate arms to alleviate fatigue.

STEP 3: Use a vent or tunnel brush on your semi-dry hair. Lift it from underneath while continuing to point the directional nozzle at the area you are brushing. These brushes have widely spaced plastic bristles that prevent thick hair from tangling and holes in the base that allow air to circulate through the hair. This speeds up the process and results in a smooth, sleek, but gently rounded, line.

BEST CUT: Unless you prefer a blunt style, thick hair requires some sort of layering to provide movement, or it will be too heavy when it falls.

PROBLEM: CURLY HAIR; NEEDS TO BE TAMED.

STEP 1: After shampooing, comb your hair with a wide-tooth comb.

STEP 2: Use a diffuser attachment. Letting your hair dry naturally is best, but a diffuser (an open, circular cone that fits over the barrel of the dryer) will at least spread the air out over a wide area so that the curls are left intact and devoid of frizz.

BEST CUT: Moderately layered. Since curly hair gets shorter as it dries, too many layers means that the top and bottom of the hair will dry to different lengths and the style will become too graduated.

Q&A

FM: What's the best style tip you ever got, and from whom?
HH: The late stylist Suga introduced me to big pin curls as a way to have soft, natural waves.

FM: What is the worst fashion faux pas?
HH: Untended roots.

FM: Who is film's most fashionable leading lady?
HH: Nicole Kidman, because she can embody a variety of fashion, hair, and make-up styles.

How to Find
the Right Moisturizer

by Evelyn H. Lauder of The Estée Lauder Companies

Evelyn H. Lauder, senior corporate vice president of The Estée Lauder Companies Inc., is a talented photographer, ardent activist, and philanthropist, as well as a devoted wife, mother, and grandmother. Born in Vienna and a survivor of the London blitz, she came to the United States with her parents and, after marrying Leonard A. Lauder, was persuaded to join the family business by her mother-in-law, Mrs. Estée Lauder. During her 45 years with the company, Evelyn Lauder has added colors and treatment products to The Estée Lauder Companies' brands while developing a reputation as a true "nose" in the fragrance industry.

The most popular and very often the first skin care product a woman purchases is a moisturizer for the face. But the product choices these days are many, and their differences can be confusing. Years ago, it used to be all about oily, normal/combination, or dry skin types. Today, however, it's not a one-size-fits-all world of moisturizers, but rather a custom fit for your skin's well-being. Here's my guide to finding the products that are right for you.

STEP 1: Take into consideration the elements that affect skin.

- **Age:** In your twenties, you need products with a higher SPF to protect your skin from future damage. In your thirties, look for hydrating products that address fine lines in the eye area. For your forties, anti-aging and repair products impart elasticity and glow and diminish deeper lines. In your fifties and sixties, use ultra-rich, deeply moisturizing creams to treat thinning skin surface and intense dryness.
- **Climate:** Use lighter moisturizers for summer and warm, moist climates; use a richer moisturizer in wintertime and in cold, dry climates.

- **Lifestyle:** Are you stressed? Do you exercise? Do you get enough sleep? How's your diet? To understand how specific behavior affects your skin, pick a time when your skin is looking its best and try to recreate the circumstances that brought it about. Were you sleeping more? Drinking less? Exercising?
- **Environment:** Pollution and sun exposure are natural enemies of the skin, so you must cleanse skin daily and use a daytime product with an appropriate SPF.

STEP 2: Determine your main skin care concern. Is it visible signs of aging from excessive sun exposure? Is it surface imperfections like flakiness or lines and wrinkles? Is it sagging and dark shadows under the eyes? Are you noticing a loss of elasticity?

STEP 3: Put yourself in the hands of someone who understands how to help you find a product that reflects those personal needs. Although I cannot speak for every person working in skin care today, we make the education of our beauty advisors a top priority. Focus your search on larger department store beauty counters or specialty stores to find the right person who understands and can accommodate your needs.

STEP 4: Sample the product. That little dab that you try on the back of your hand at the counter can tell you a lot! Do you like the texture? The absorbency rate? The way it smells? Does it leave your skin silky? Smooth? Ask for a sample size to try over a period of days at home.

STEP 5: Apply the moisturizer you selected twice a day on clean, dry skin. Use an upward circular motion, working across your face and then lightly stroke downward, to flatten fine hairs. Don't forget your neck and décolletage.

It All Begins with Good Skin Care

Here is my personal routine:

- **Cleanse thoroughly.** No matter how tired I am, I never, ever go to bed or get up in the morning without cleansing my face.

- **Follow with a gentle peel or refinisher.** A skin refinisher helps perfect the surface of the skin and reduces imperfections, such as flakiness, redness, uneven skin tone, pores, and fine lines. Refinishers also help balance skin by adjusting skin's moisture content and oil production. These can be used twice a week and offer a gentle at-home alternative to microdermabrasion.

- **Apply a line prevention serum.** This is the number one skin care concern today. Look for gentle, retinol-free correcting serums that reduce the look of fine, dry lines instantly. These products can help your skin look luminous and feel velvety-smooth.

- **Repair.** Products that help repair past damage and prevent visible signs of aging are an absolute must in my routine. They can significantly reduce the look of existing lines and prevent future signs of aging. Skin will look younger, healthier, and less lined by using these repair serums morning and night.

- **Moisturize.** The main objective of moisturizers is to keep skin comfortable, provide protection, and improve skin's appearance. Today's moisturizers are multitaskers! They help create a perfectly controlled climate for your skin that adapts it to the multiple causes of dehydration.

STEP 6: Target your eyes. I strongly recommend using a product specifically designed for this delicate area, because the skin around the eye is thinner and more vulnerable than other areas of the face, with few oil glands. Moisturizers for the eye area are specially formulated to hydrate, protect, and repair the delicate skin. They also address the most typical eye care concerns: lines, loss of firmness, darkness, and puffiness.

⚠ **"I need to look fresh—fast."** Before you go out in the evening, especially if you need to go straight from work, pat a little matte eye cream under the eyes and over makeup to soften wrinkles and refresh your whole look. Be gentle, and pat, never rub. Excess eye cream also can be used around the lips. If it's good for your eyes, it's certainly good for your lips!

Q&A

FM: Define "timeless."
EL: Beauty is timeless, and the goal is not to look good for your age but to look good at your age. My mother-in-law, Estée Lauder, often said that the most beautiful face in the world is your own.

FM: What are the worst fashion faux pas?
EL: Pantylines, a white bra with a white blouse (always wear nude), miniskirts after a certain age, and knee socks at any age.

FM: Define "fashion forward."
EL: Wearing bright and clashing colors, like a light blue suit with a poison green T-shirt—these colors sing to me.

How to Get and Keep Smooth Skin

by Jennifer and Sara Jaqua of Jaqua Beauty

Jennifer and Sara Jaqua grew up on the beach in Santa Barbara and often gathered their girlfriends for "Beauty Parlor Nights" to manicure, pedicure, exfoliate, and polish using Mom's priciest potions. Fittingly, the sisters started Jaqua Beauty in 1997 with a "Beauty Parlor Night Kit" that was featured on Oprah. They still believe that getting women together for pampering sessions is the best way to spend time. Jaqua products are fun to use, smell wonderful, and are among the most effective on the market.

For many women, facial skin care products take precedence over body skin care products because we see the face first. But once the face draws someone in, you need sexy arms and legs and other body parts. You want beauty beyond the book cover, and focusing on the entire body takes skin care to a whole other level.

Exfoliation removes the dead skin cells that make the skin look dull and feel rough. The friction also boosts your circulation and helps unclog pores. This is more than a cosmetic concern: Increasing your blood circulation also stimulates your lymphatic system, which in turn helps to detoxify your body. Our skin is the largest organ that eliminates toxins on a daily basis. If our skin is not healthy, we put a burden on our lymphatic system and other organs. We suggest that you exfoliate your skin at least once a week.

STEP 1: Get your skin thoroughly wet. We prefer the shower over the bath because you can stand in the spray and cover more surface area.

STEP 2: Turn off the water and apply an exfoliation product to your wet skin, starting with the feet and working your way up. Use your bare hands to give you more control of the product, so you can feel exactly where you are placing it and push it into the skin. Cream-based nut scrubs (with jojoba beads) have the benefit of covering more surface, but because the granules are smaller, they are more suited to facial exfoliation. Scrubs for the body should have coarser particles (like sea salt and sugar) and contain more natural oils. Not only do they exfoliate well, their oil base will nourish and hydrate the skin, too. For skin that is extremely dry and scaly, moisturizers or creams containing salicylic or lactic acid can help.

STEP 3: Thoroughly rinse the exfoliating product from your skin.

STEP 4: While your skin is still damp, apply an oil-based body moisturizer so that the oil is absorbed by the skin and is retained longer. By applying moisturizer while your skin is wet, you help "trap" moisture. Your exfoliated skin should feel soft, smooth, and moisturized. And it should glow.

⚠ **"I have these weird little red bumps on the back of my upper arms."** Those little red surface bumps (resembling goose bumps) that can appear on the back of your upper arms are *pilaris*, and they are caused by dry skin getting stuck in pores. Preventing pilaris requires a combination of regular exfoliation and moisturizing, and a hydrating sugar scrub is great for removing them. Remember to exfoliate gently on arms where bumps appear so you don't irritate sensitive skin.

FM: Define "timeless."

JJ/SJ: Classic and timeless is always better, because it's much less painful to look back at old pictures of yourself without wondering what in the world you were thinking!

FM: What's the best style tip you ever got, and from whom?

JJ/SJ: Expensive and well-styled accessories will make even a boring outfit shine—from our German aunt who learned to be a tailor in the fashionable city of Düsseldorf.

FM: Who is film's most fashionable leading lady?

JJ/SJ: Catherine Deneuve. Because her style is classic and her beauty is legendary.

EXTRA HELP

Daily Moisturizing

Always keep a stash of moisturizers in your car, office, and by your bed. To achieve highly moisturized skin we recommend the following:

- Use a dry oil spray, preferably one that contains meadow foam seed oil (more than 98 percent long-chain fatty acids and with higher quality triglyceride levels compared with other vegetable oils). Because of its small molecular size, it quickly penetrates into the skin and absorbs quickly without becoming greasy.

- Add a weekly moisturizing bath to your beauty regimen. Put a few tablespoons of powdered milk (which contains natural beta hydroxy acids to exfoliate and soothe skin) into a warm tub. Add a capful of a hydrating bath oil or bath gel for increased moisturizing benefits.

HOW TO DEAL WITH A BLEMISH

by Cornelia Zicu of Cornelia Day Resort

Romanian-born aesthetician Cornelia Zicu has established herself as the master of instinctive and healing touch by combining her grandmother's natural remedies with hands-on experience. After launching her New York career at the Spa at the Peninsula Hotel, Zicu consulted in the development of the Peter Thomas Roth and June Jacobs skin care lines. In 2004, she opened Cornelia, her own state-of-the art spa on the top two floors of the Ferragamo flagship building in midtown Manhattan.

A blemish can be caused by any one of several factors, from hormone disorders and touching the face with dirty hands to using the wrong skin care products and/or receiving treatments that are not appropriate for one's skin type. If you are prone to blemishes, contact a specialist or skin care expert. But if you only get an occasional blemish, you can handle it on your own—as long as you stay focused on antibacterial and anti-inflammatory treatments that lead to healing. *This does not include squeezing!* Squeezing a blemish or pimple on your own could traumatize the skin and leave permanent damage. You might even inflame the blemish and create an area for the bacteria to grow, multiplying and spreading the problem.

STEP 1: Wash your hands. Your hands must always be clean when you touch your face, so washing them well is the first and most important step.

STEP 2: Delicately use a cleanser on the blemished area twice a day, morning and night. Don't scrub the spot—wash it gently.

STEP 3: Once the area is clean, apply an astringent. The best astringents have mint, eucalyptus, chamomile, or salicylic acid, all of which have antibacterial proprieties. Use a large round cotton pad (not ball). These discs (about 2½ inches [6 cm] in diameter) have a slightly quilted surface so they don't "fuzz" like regular cotton balls—those microscopic fibers from cotton balls can adhere to a blemish and actually add to the infection. Place the cotton pad across the middle fingers of your hand (palm side up) and hold it flat by tucking the edges under your little finger and index finger. Dampen the surface with astringent and wipe your face (including your neck) with long, smooth strokes.

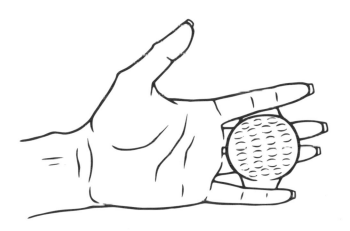

STEP 4: Apply a dab of a facial mask. Use a mask with camphor, mint, eucalyptus, magnesium, or copper as an ingredient, for its disinfectant and healing properties. Although masks are most effective when used as a weekly or biweekly treatment, you can also target the blemished area specifically. The area immediately around the blemish should not be treated with moisturizer, as it will only exacerbate the spreading of bacteria.

STEP 5: Apply a blemish treatment product, then apply a concealer if you are feeling self-conscious or have an important date. When used with a pimple treatment product, concealer can help to cover up a blemish, but it should never be applied directly to a blemish. Always apply a blemish treatment product first, let it dry, and then layer on your concealer and then foundation—but only if you clean the area well before going to bed.

⚠ **"The hot weather is making my face break out."** Everyone's skin is more prone to blemishes in hot, humid weather, because the moist, hot air provides the ideal conditions for bacteria growth. The best and cheapest disinfectant is an ice cube. Just as cold weather disinfects the atmosphere, running a cube of ice wrapped in gauze or a paper towel over your face kills bacteria and improves the skin's circulation. So will washing your face with cool, not hot, water.

Q&A

FM: What's the best style tip you ever got, and from whom?
CZ: My mother told me that posture is key. Good posture can make an average outfit look fantastic; bad posture can make a fantastic outfit look just average.

FM: Who is your favorite style icon?
CZ: Coco Chanel invented style.

FM: What is your favorite fashion scene from a movie?
CZ: I love the scene in *Pretty Woman* where Julia Roberts attends the polo match wearing her large straw hat and ladylike dress. Her triumphant spirit makes her stand out.

Applying Facial Masks

Many people misinterpret the tightening power of a mud or clay mask as "cleansing," but the drying action can send the wrong message to the skin. Instead of creating balance, the body can produce even more oil to counteract the skin's surface dryness. These masks also pull the skin as they tighten—particularly in more delicate areas—and can cause tiny broken capillaries.

I prefer to use a cream or gel mask (with a consistency like sour cream) that won't harden but will still remain in place on the skin. For those who are "firm" believers in a mud or clay product, I suggest spraying the face with water (or using a damp compress) to keep the mask moist and prevent the drying, tightening action. You will still receive the benefits of the active ingredients, even if the mud or clay base doesn't tighten.

How to Maintain
a Shapely Brow

by Robin Narvaez of Borja Color Studio

After receiving her cosmetology and aesthetician's licenses, New York City–born-and-bred Robin Narvaez joined the International Alliance of Theatrical Stage Employees (I.A.T.S.E.), a labor union of creative artists in the film industry, and began a career as a makeup artist for film and print, including work for Oprah, Vogue, *and* Allure. *When not on the set, Narvaez is based at Borja Color Studio, where she was named the only five-star makeup artist in* New York *magazine's "Test Drive: Face Facts," as well as "Best Brow Shaper 2004."*

Shaping eyebrows used to be a job left to specific aestheticians, typically those who also did manicures. Then the whole world finally figured out that eyebrows are in the middle of your face and can change your features. Now people who shouldn't even have tweezers are wielding them. Eyebrows have become part of a beauty assembly line. But there is no one brow shape. Take that old fifties shaping rule about placing a pencil in the corner of your eye and rotating it to measure where the beginning, middle, and end of your brow should go—well, today arches no longer go over the center of your eye. Arches go where nature puts them. I can't give you one-brow-fits-all advice, but here are guidelines for putting your best brow forward.

STEP 1: Ditch the wax. The skin around your eye area is 20 percent less dense than anywhere else on your body. So why would you take the thinnest tissue you have, apply hot wax (of an indeterminate temperature) to it with an ice cream stick, and then—after it opens the pores, deposits itself inside, and turns itself into a candle—rip it off?

STEP 2: Get yourself tweezers with strong spring action and pointy tips. In finding your eyebrow line, three hairs can make a difference—the precision you need is in the tweezing. Make sure your tweezers have a pointy end that can tweeze single hairs. When tweezers have a square or slanted edge, you can end up grabbing more than one hair at a time.

STEP 3: Be sure you have the proper amount of light and magnification before you begin to tweeze. Prime time for tweezing your brows is daytime, in a place where there's plenty of natural light—not in your car at the stop sign. Alternatively, use a well-lit mirror. Depending upon your level of eyesight, you can use a magnifying mirror that ranges from 3x to 10x. But remember. No matter how enlarged the view of your eye area, trying to get every single hair is what gives your brow an unnatural line. Your body is covered in hair for a reason; leave a little humanity in your eyebrow.

STEP 4: Before you tweeze, apply toner or astringent to the entire brow and surrounding skin. This doesn't just prepare the skin; it takes the moisture out of the hair so the tweezers won't slip.

STEP 5: Start tweezing under your arch and walk into your natural line. Don't start tweezing at the front of your brow, and don't fight your natural arch. What is vital to finding the arch is that the hair on top of your eyebrow is not touched. You can see how that hair crests and then begins to slope downward at the end of the brow—that determines your natural arch. Once you wax or

tweeze the hair on top of your eyebrow, your brow is no longer naturally shaped—it is manmade.

STEP 6: Tweeze in between your brows. The best rule of thumb is to use your thumb! Place one thumb on the bridge of your nose between your eyes (upside down, with your hand in front of your forehead). Observe the space covered by your thumb—do not roll your thumb from side to side. Anything under your thumb can go.

Q&A

FM: What's the worst fashion faux pas?
RN: Cookie-cutter, stenciled brows.

FM: Who is your favorite style icon?
RN: Diana Vreeland, for her fieriness and independence. She could carry off anything she put on because she "felt" it; she owned it.

FM: What is your favorite fashion scene from a movie?
RN: In *Moulin Rouge*, Nicole Kidman had these long, overextended eyebrows, and they worked so fabulously that everyone I knew started to paint in the back of their brows.

Groom Your Brows

For grooming, use a clean, soft, flat-bristle toothbrush and always brush your eyebrows in the direction the hair grows. That doesn't just mean up. Follow the shape, and resist the temptation to trim unruly hairs. Eyebrow hair is not like head hair. When you cut it, it goes into shock and gets wiry.

If your brows are extra thick and unruly, don't try to control them with hairspray or other hair care products. Many such products contain alcohol and fragrance and can irritate the sensitive eye area. Use a clear mascara "brow tamer" instead: Just about every cosmetic line makes one, and they come complete with an application wand.

How to Apply False Eyelashes

by Jim Crawford for Revlon

Jim Crawford is a leading editorial makeup artist with 20 years in the business. He is sought after for red carpet events and as a beauty industry expert, regularly appearing on E! and the Style Channel.

False eyelashes, invented in 1916 by director D. W. Griffith as a beauty enhancement for actress Seena Owen in his film *Intolerance*, add drama to any eye shape. Flirtatious, feminine, and ultra-glamorous, lashes are the perfect accent to an evening look. There are two types of false eyelashes: (1) full lashes, which come in strips, add density to the entire lash line, and must be trimmed to fit the width of your eyelid, and (2) individual lashes, which come in little clusters and can be used to fill in sparse areas.

FOR FULL LASHES

STEP 1: Apply concealer to the under-eye area to mask any discoloration (purplish appearance) and even out your skin tone. Dab the product to the under-eye and the lower lash line with your fingers. Your fingers' warmth will melt the product, making it easier to apply.

STEP 2: Gently work a small amount of concealer into the upper lid (where the skin is thin and sensitive) to eliminate any veins or discoloration. Concealer provides a great base for shadow and prolongs the life of eye makeup. If you are going to wear shadow, apply it now.

STEP 3: Hold the lashes to your upper lid to measure the width. If necessary, use small scissors to trim the lashes, working in from the outer corner.

STEP 4: Holding the lash with your fingertips, curl the lashes gently with an eyelash curler.

STEP 5: If using a nonadhesive lash, carefully apply transparent eyelash glue to the lash. Self-adhesive lashes are easier to trim to size and apply, but if you are using the nonadhesive type, place a dab of the glue on the back of your hand and use a small toothpick to apply the glue to the lash. Allow the glue to set. I always hold the lash up to a warm light bulb to speed up the process.

STEP 6: Apply the lash. Here's a great tip: Hold a hand mirror below your chin and look down as you apply so that you lay the lash in at the correct angle. Place the lash in the middle of the eye, above the iris, and work the lash into the inner and outer corners. Hold for a few seconds to secure. If you are using a self-adhesive lash, hold it in place for several seconds and then gently tug to ensure placement.

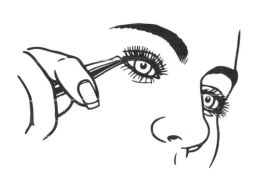

FOR INDIVIDUAL LASHES

Individual lashes are great for masking small bare spots. Generally available in three sizes (flare short, medium, and long), you need about seven to eight "clusters" to achieve a full, natural look. I usually cut full self-adhesive lashes into small sections to achieve this look. Individual lashes that must be glued are harder to apply and require patience and a steady hand.

STEP 1: Apply concealer as directed in steps 1 and 2 on page 42.

STEP 2: Place a small amount of glue on the back of your hand. Remove individual clusters from the lash tray with tweezers and use a toothpick to place the glue on the lash. Let the glue set before you place it on the lash line: you can employ the same light bulb trick from step 5, on page 43.

STEP 3: Apply lash clusters 1 to 2 millimeters apart and as close to your natural lash line as possible. Use tweezers to work inward from the outer corner of your eye. (It usually takes 7 or 8 clusters.) Don't be discouraged—practice makes perfect. This can be tricky even for makeup pros!

STEP 4: Carefully curl your lashes. Using a lash curler, curl your lashes gently and carefully so you don't release the clusters.

⚠ **"I've come undone!"** If you are wearing false lashes, it is always a good idea to arm yourself with a tube of lash glue in your makeup or evening bag. The last thing you want is for one of your eyelashes to wind up in your date's salad. If your lash has released itself at one of the ends (but has not completely come off), use a small eyeliner brush or flat toothpick with a miniscule amount of glue on it to reaffix.

FM: What's the best style tip you ever received, and from whom?

JC: Radiate confidence! I've been fortunate to work with some of the world's most recognized women, from Isabella Rossellini to Maggie Gyllenhaal. They are self assured, sexy, and embrace their individuality.

FM: What's the worst fashion faux pas?

JC: Matching your lipstick, mani/pedi, eye shadow, etc. to your outfit. Adding color to your wardrobe is great, but if you're wearing a jacket in a strong color like red, use that shade sparingly in your beauty look. Instead of red lips, nails, and toes, try pairing a gorgeous sheer red lip and a subtle pink mani/pedi. The same rule applies for accessories. It's a much more modern approach, and you won't look too "matchy matchy."

FM: What is your favorite scene from a movie?

JC: Fashion icon Audrey Hepburn, in *Breakfast at Tiffany's* was a showcase for glamour and elegance. Her makeup, hair, and wardrobe were fashion forward and flawless.

EXTRA HELP

Applying Mascara

Once the lash is firmly in place, you are ready to apply the finishing touch: mascara. Gently apply the mascara with upward strokes, starting at the lash line. This will allow the natural lashes to bond with the false. Eyeliner is optional, but works well to disguise the false lash line (which can be a little less visible on a self-adhesive lash). Now au revoir, double kiss—you're ready to flaunt look-at-me lashes.

HOW TO BECOME YOUR OWN MAKEUP ARTIST®

by Paula Dorf of Paula Dorf Cosmetics

As a child, Paula Dorf was fascinated by her mother's daily makeup ritual; as an adult, she found her calling as a makeup artist for television, film, and the fashion runway. Today, her cosmetics and hand-cut brushes designed to fit every angle of a woman's face are sold in specialty stores and department stores such as Bloomingdales; they are used by hundreds of television and film makeup artists, as well as by every woman who wants to become her own makeup artist.

On film sets during my years as a makeup artist, I carted around enough brushes and makeup to fill a tackle box. Since every job and every face was different, I never knew what problems I would encounter. There also just weren't any quality brushes designed to fit every angle of a woman's face.

And so I began my quest to design the ultimate brush set. I went to art supply stores and cut and shaped the brushes to fit the task. I tested each brush on the actors, who were amazed at the difference a great brush can make. Soon I was making custom brush sets for some of today's most famous faces.

Great brushes are the key to applying makeup, because they enhance color application so it looks better and lasts longer. The proper makeup brush collection can be more important than the makeup itself.

HOW TO CHOOSE YOUR BRUSHES

This basic kit is a good place to start on your way to becoming your own makeup artist.

FERRULE: This metal band joins the bristles to the handle. It should be well made and secure, holding the bristles neatly. Grasp the bristles of the brush in one hand and tug gently. Nothing should escape the ferrule.

HANDLE: I prefer a wooden handle to plastic for the craftsmanship and the feel. Gently grip the handle as you would a pencil to give you the control you need.

TUFT: I use brushes of natural hair (like sable and squirrel) or Taklon, an extremely high-grade manmade nylon fiber. Taklon bristles have better release, reducing the amount of product you need and providing you with better control. Taklon is easy to clean, so you can avoid the bacterial buildup that comes with using a cosmetic sponge. For application of powder products (like eye shadow or powder blush), the microscopically uneven surface of natural bristles picks up and holds particles best. Blue squirrel hair bristles are the finest hair available for powder.

HAIR LENGTH: The length of the brush hair changes the intensity of makeup application. The shorter the brush hair, the more dramatic the look; longer brush hair creates a sheer application.

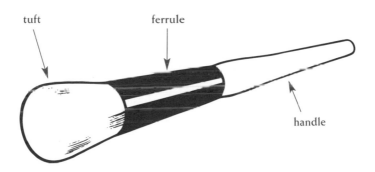

SHAPE: Brushes typically come in three bristle shapes: straight, chiseled (or graduated), and tapered. Straight brushes make straight lines (e.g., for applying eyeliner), tapered brushes can handle curves (e.g., for lining your lips); and chiseled or graduated brushes are good for spreading and blending (e.g., for applying products like foundation).

CARE: Quality brushes should last a lifetime. I still use my original set! Many makeup lines also make brush cleaners. Look for one that has natural cleansing agents, is gentle to the skin, alcohol free, and hypoallergenic.

HOW TO USE THE CONCEALER BRUSH

A concealer brush is designed to blend concealer evenly and prevent streaking. It should be flat, with Taklon bristles that have a rounded or domed top so the brush fits in the corner of the eye and against the bridge of the nose. Since the goal of concealer is to minimize imperfection (not cover it up), the color should be in line with your skin tone. Be careful not to go too light! You can match your concealer perfectly by testing the color on your jawbone.

STEP 1: Lightly press both sides of the brush into the concealer, bearing in mind that only a small amount of product is needed. If you apply too much concealer, it will draw attention to the area rather than divert the eye.

STEP 2: Use the full face of the tuft to gently pat the product into your skin. Resist the temptation to sweep the brush back and forth—continue gently pressing the brush against the skin, depositing product evenly until it is no longer visible. This application technique will hold true regardless of your concealing needs: unsightly blemishes, bluish tones, veins, or discoloration. For under the eye, start in the corner near the brow bone, working only to the area directly below your pupil.

STEP 3: Lightly feather the product to avoid that telltale "debarkation" concealer line.

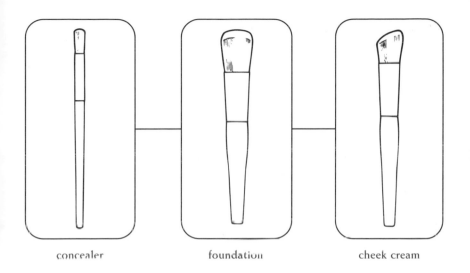

concealer foundation cheek cream

HOW TO USE THE FOUNDATION BRUSH

The foundation brush is flat with a rounded or domed tip to give you the most natural, even coverage when applying liquid foundation. It should have fine, soft Taklon bristles and be chiseled (or graduated) so you can get into every crease.

STEP 1: Find your ideal foundation by matching the color of the product to your neck, not your face. The skin in these areas is of a slightly different hue. Since you will not be putting foundation on your neck, that's your base hue, and you don't want your face to be a different color.

STEP 2: Place a dollop of foundation in the palm of one hand and apply it to both sides of the brush.

STEP 3: Use the full face of the tuft to press the foundation into your skin. Work your way from each side of your nose, across each cheekbone, and down to your chin.

STEP 4: Now use the same technique to cover your nose and forehead, blending with small, light strokes.

HOW TO USE THE CHEEK CREAM (BLUSH) BRUSH

The Taklon brush you use to apply cream blush should be made of fine, chiseled (or graduated) soft bristles, gently angled on one side to fit the "apple" of your cheek (the rounded area under the middle of the eye). The color of cream blush is more intense than a powder, but creams also have more emollients, so they are easier to blend.

STEP 1: Apply product to both sides of the tuft.

STEP 2: Look into the mirror and smile in an exaggerated manner.

STEP 3: Using the full face of the brush, with the angled side toward your nose, pat the cream blush onto the center of the "apples" that appear.

STEP 4: With quick, light strokes, sweep the blush up toward your hairline, but do not go past the corner of your eye.

HOW TO USE THE SHEER CREASE BRUSH

This barrel-shaped brush should have dense, soft, natural bristles (like blue squirrel) tapered to fit the eye crease. The eye contour color is applied on the bone directly above the crease.

STEP 1: Dip the brush into the powdered shadow and tap off the excess. Blowing on the brush only scatters the little grains of powder everywhere and wastes product.

STEP 2: Start at the outside corner of your eye and gently use a windshield-wiper motion to apply the product. Never extend the color past the end of your brow. Since you want a soft and even wash of color, avoid swiping the brush back and forth and lifting it between strokes (as though you are painting a wall). The brush should not lose contact with the skin.

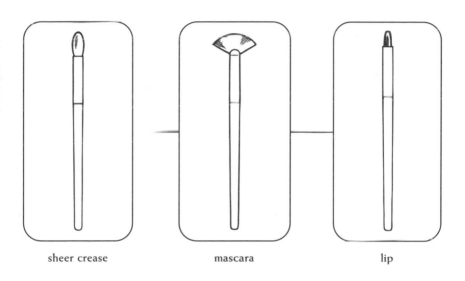

sheer crease   mascara   lip

HOW TO USE THE MASCARA FAN

A mascara fan is flat, with Taklon bristles of a slightly heavy and firm weight. The tuft is splayed (like an open fan) and the light, long handle gives better control than a conventional mascara wand, for better separation and more complete coverage.

STEP 1: Transfer mascara to the fan brush by swiping the brush back and forth along the mascara wand.

STEP 2: Apply the mascara starting at the root of your eyelashes, coating them to thicken without clumping.

HOW TO USE THE LIP BRUSH

A lip brush should be flat, with tapered Taklon bristles that have a rounded tip for precise application.

STEP 1: Swipe the brush back and forth on the lipstick to saturate the bristles with color.

STEP 2: Press the full side of the brush on your lips to deposit and lock in color, then blend the lipstick with small, light strokes.

STEP 3: Finish by using the edge of the brush to outline your lips. Doing this last eliminates a harsh lip line, yet still provides definition.

Q&A

FM: What's the best style tip you ever got, and from whom?
PD: "Powder and paint make you what you ain't," from my mom.

FM: What's the worst fashion faux pas?
PD: Too much blush and blush that is poorly blended.

FM: Define "fashion forward."
PD: Everything comes full circle: shoes go from round to pointy to square and back again. The same goes for makeup—for example, cake mascara was huge in the '50s and is now popular again.

How to Make a Smoky Eye

by Jeanine Lobell of Stila Cosmetics

Educated in London, Swedish-born Jeanine Lobell moved to Los Angeles and began her career doing makeup for music videos, magazine covers, and award shows. After developing makeup products for a small boutique, she founded Stila, a line of easy-to-use, high-quality products in gorgeous, fun packaging. Trends in pop culture, music, and fashion shows play a major role in the creation of Stila's new shades and products, and today Stila Cosmetics are available internationally.

The one look my friends always ask me to teach them is the smoky eye. They kind of sneak up to me and shyly ask, as if they are asking me to divulge a secret sex technique. It's amusing that the smoky eye has such a forbidden-fruit quality for some women. It's not only a great nighttime "come-hither" look—with the right colors it's also a sophisticated daytime option.

STEP 1: Determine the shade of the shadow. More natural shades (like browns, taupes, and grays) will look softer; non–skin tone shades (like greens, blues, and plums) will look more apparent on the face. The choice is yours, but if you are a beginner, you might want to stick to medium-browns and taupes

Consider your skin tone—if your skin is light, choose a lighter version of a shadow color (like a lighter plum); the deeper your skin, the darker you need to go (like an aubergine). A swatch test on the back of your hand will help you decide the best shade for you.

STEP 2: Choose texture: matte or shimmer. A light shimmer shadow is much easier to work with, as it will blend more subtly into the skin. Mattes look great, but require a little more skill.

STEP 3: Use the flat end of a small, double-ended shadow brush to apply a base shadow all over the lid area. Your base shadow should be a neutral, matte shadow that will act as a primer or foundation before you apply the colored shadow. It will help the color shadow grab on and stay put, and it will also neutralize your eyelid's natural skin tone so the color of the shadow on your lid will more closely match its color in the pan.

STEP 4: Pick up a little of the colored shadow with the flat end of your double-sided eye shadow brush. Blend the shadow from the upper lash line up into the crease to open and lift the eye.

STEP 5: Use the pointy end of the brush to apply the colored shadow to the lower lash line. Begin your application in the center of the lower lash line, just below the iris. Move the brush slowly from side to side to give you more control in placement, so you can catch any over-shading.

Smoky liner under the eye will make your eyes look bigger, but it can also exaggerate flaws like close-set eyes or droopy corners. For close-set eyes, don't go too far into the inner corners. For droopy eyes, keep the line extra thin in the outer corners, widening in the center and toward the inner corners.

STEP 6: Experiment with the thickness of the line below the eye. If you get a hang-dog look, take a Q-tip and lift up the line. Remember, the key is not to have a hard, solid line; the more smudged and broken the better. You can even take your finger and blend-smudge the line if it looks too solid. Once you have learned what placement works best for you, it's a breeze. You can play with different colors, moving from soft taupes to subtle khakis.

STEP 7: If you prefer a little extra definition, use the pointy end of your double-sided brush to add a shadow on the top lash line. Choose a color that is a step darker than your lid color, but still within the same color family.

STEP 8: Always finish this look with a generous helping of mascara on the top and bottom lashes.

Q&A

FM: Define "timeless."
JL: A black cashmere turtleneck.

FM: What's the best style tip you ever got, and from whom?
JL: My dad says you can always get away with any sloppy outfit as long as you wear good shoes.

FM: What's your favorite fashion scene from a movie?
JL: The day Julia Roberts goes shopping on Rodeo Drive in *Pretty Woman*.

How to Go Glossy

by Anna Lisa Raya and Belén Aranda-Alvarado of Wink Beauty

Wink Beauty founders Anna Lisa Raya and Belén Aranda-Alvarado discovered the pleasures of lip lining, eyelash curling, and brow-bone highlighting as interns at Elle *magazine. A Harvard Business School graduate, Aranda-Alvarado's work at* Latina *magazine inspired her to write* Latina Beauty, *the first beauty book written for the U.S. Hispanic market. Raya got her M.S. from the Columbia Graduate School of Journalism before working at* People *maga-zine and as fashion editor of* Movieline. *She is currently on staff at* Variety.

When it comes to a "look," there are a few important accessories and beauty items that can transform a person: a statement-making handbag or exquisite shoes, or an eyelash curler and mascara that open up the eyes in unbelievable ways. Lip gloss is one of those essential tools. More than lipstick, lip gloss has the power to be the first thing you notice on a person when she enters a room. Most of this has to do with the shine factor—that's what makes gloss sexy, and it's also what helps plump up the lips without any of those trendy "lip-pumping" ingredients.

STEP 1: If you're experiencing some dryness, prime your lips for gloss by massaging a little lip balm over them and then blotting off the excess. Be careful: Too much balm on your lips will dilute your gloss's pig-ment and longevity.

STEP 2: If you want your lip gloss to stay on as long as possible, line your lips, and then fill them in with liner before glossing. This will also help min-imize feathering. Liner can be used to accent or deepen your color as well as to give you a more defined look. Pick a complementary shade and apply. There are three ways to go: along the natural lip line, just inside the lip line, and just outside the lip line. Staying inside the line will make lips appear slightly smaller; going outside does the opposite. The best way is to just keep it natural. (Too often we see women who draw lip liner way past the natural lip line and they end up looking clownish.)

STEP 3: Apply the gloss in layers. Applying lip gloss is pretty self-explanatory, but some glosses also have the ability to layer very well. If you just apply a light first coat, the pigment will remain subtle. If you keep applying layers of gloss, much the same way you do with mascara, you'll get to a color that pops off the lips. Lip gloss is also fun to layer over other colors or even lipstick. Use your gloss to punch some shimmer into an old matte lipstick you have lying around.

STEP 4: Give yourself a little sexy pout for a finishing touch. Dab a bit of light, shimmery lip gloss (something with a gold or silver hue works best) in the center of your bottom lip. This is a tried and true beauty trick that all the pros use.

⚠ **"My lips are too flaky!"** Moisten your lips with water or lip balm, then run an old, softened toothbrush over your lips. Don't bother with the lip balms that are made with exfoliating beads. Those never work as well as a good ol' toothbrush.

FM: Define "timeless."

ALA/BAA: Red lips. We'll take 'em glossy, matte, or creamy—it doesn't matter. Nothing is so simple, yet sophisticated, as red lips. The trick is deciding if you're a warm-tone red or a cool-tone red, but once that part is figured out, pretty much any woman looks classic in red.

FM: What is the worst fashion faux pas?

ALA/BAA: Lips lined with dark, brownish liner pencil and topped with sheer gloss. We don't know where this look started or when, but it has never looked good on anyone.

FM: Who is your favorite style icon?

ALA/BAA: Anna Wintour, editor in chief of American *Vogue*, for always sticking with a signature look: the bob, the sunglasses, the sweater set—full skirt—Manolo Blahnik outfits she wears day to day.

How to Choose a Gloss

Keep these essentials in mind when making your choice.

- **Consistency**: Look for gloss that has a balmy, creamy consistency; it should feel emollient, not sticky.

- **Pigment**: Good lip gloss should have some color to it—an even, vibrant wash. But beware of brands with too much pigment; you end up having to blot them down.

- **Scent**: Unscented gloss tends to smell chemically, whereas some scented glosses can be saccharine sweet. Choose a smart gloss that has scent only on application and won't overwhelm you or others nearby.

- **Application**: Lip gloss should always come with its own applicator. What woman wants to stick her finger into a pot of lip gloss? A brush is great, but it won't yield as much control as an angled, "doe foot" sponge-tip applicator.

- **Longevity**: If a gloss has a good creamy base and a thorough, though not overpowering, pigment, it should last at least an hour on your lips. Gloss that's reapplied every hour or so will always keep a woman looking refreshed and put together.

How to Find the Right Frames for Your Face

by Selima Salaun of Selima Optique

Algerian-born Selima Salaun has been at the forefront of fashionable eyewear for more than ten years, ushering in an era of color and new looks. A Paris-trained licensed optician and optometrist, Salaun moved to New York City and opened Selima Optique Soho, which quickly became a favored destination for style mavens like Winona Ryder, Donatella Versace, and Bono. Salaun now has shops in New York, Los Angeles, and Paris, and her collection of handmade frames—Selima Optique—is sold worldwide.

There's a reason actors use different eyeglasses to go in and out of character: The frames we wear say something about who we are. Frames do more than "frame" the face and bring attention to the eyes; eyeglasses reflect personality. Since your glasses are the first thing that people notice about you, selecting the right pair is not an impulse purchase. Set aside time to shop, and patronize a store where the salespeople are adept at helping you to select the right frames.

You will undoubtedly see a lot of "designer" frames when shopping. But more important than the brand is the expertise of the salesperson who will find frames to complement your face's shape and skin tone.

Your eyeglasses should not only fit your face but also fit your life. I recommend four pairs: a style for (1) work, (2) exercise, (3) evening, and (4) sunglasses. I am always surprised by women who have fifty pairs of shoes and only one pair of eyeglasses.

STEP 1: Present your current prescription to your salesperson. Not all styles of glasses work with all prescriptions. Ask if there are any restrictions on the frames you can select.

STEP 2: Tell the salesperson a bit about your personal style. Describe yourself, your job, and your style preferences, so he or she can get a sense of what frames might fit into your life.

STEP 3: Have the salesperson consider your features. A trained salesperson will consider your eyes, nose, and cheekbones as a blueprint to selecting frames that will balance the shape of your face. It is all about proportion:

- **Round-shaped faces** (with the greatest width at the cheekbones) do well with wider, horizontal eyeglasses that are slightly angular. Choose rectangular frames that are straight across the top and bottom to give the illusion of length and cheekbones.
- **Oval-shaped faces** (with the forehead slightly wider than the chin) can carry off almost any frame, since the structure of the face is relatively balanced both vertically and horizontally. Choose a pair with a bit wider bridge; avoid small frames that make your face look even longer.
- **Square-shaped faces** (a bit "boxy," with a strong jaw line) should be softened with round, oval, or cats' eye shapes that draw attention away from the jaw line to the top of the frames.
- **Heart-shaped faces** (with forehead significantly wider than chin) are best balanced by frames that draw attention away from the forehead and down toward the chin, like ovals or rectangular frames with curved bottom rims.

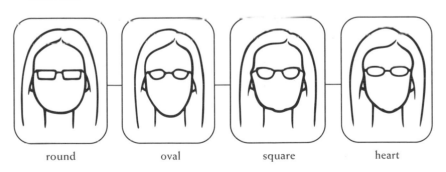

round   oval   square   heart

Frame Fit Considerations

It is important to remember that style is secondary to fit, and buying a pair of eyeglasses that doesn't fit you properly is like buying shoes that don't quite fit. They may look great but are ultimately so uncomfortable that you can't wear them for any length of time without doing some sort of damage. A pair of badly adjusted eyeglasses can actually cause migraines. Here are some factors to keep in mind as you make your selection.

- Consider the weight of the frames without lenses. They should rest lightly but securely on your nose, with no discomfort.

- The frames must fit the bridge of the nose snugly but without pinching. Like a bridge that joins two pieces of land, the bridge of your frames is responsible for evenly distributing the weight of the eyeglasses.

- The temple (or arm) should rest lightly on the top of the ear and, if curved, should follow the shape of the ear and rest comfortably behind it (although this can be adjusted).

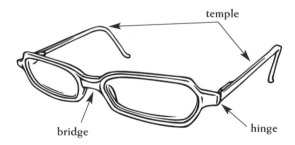

temple

bridge

hinge

STEP 4: Make sure the frames complement the color of your skin. There are two general categories of skin tone: warm and cool. "Warm" means that you have yellow undertones to your skin, and are best complemented by colors like camel, khaki, navy blue, orangey reds, off-white, and matte black. For metal frames, seek out gold, bronze, or copper. You will also look good in a golden brown or blonde tortoiseshell. "Cool" means you have blue undertones (really!), and are best complemented by colors like bright white, shiny black, plum, magenta, pink, and blue-red. Metal frames can be pewter, graphite, enameled metal, brushed, or shiny silver. You will also look good in demi-amber (darker) tortoiseshell.

STEP 5: Before you buy, try your frames on while looking in a full-length mirror. Now that you've chosen frames in a shape and color that complements your face and skin tone, you need to be sure they fit with your total look.

⚠ **"I'm not sure my frames go with my hair color."** A frame in harmony with your hair color is sure to be perfect. If hair is honey-colored/brown, tortoise frames are perfect. If your hair is gray, crystal frames are great. Navy is perfect for blue eyes (generally found on those with cool skin tones). Darker skin colors can generally wear bright colors, and women with red hair look great in green-framed eyeglasses. Don't forget to make sure that the color of your lipstick doesn't clash with the color of your eyeglass frames.

FM: Define "trendy."

SS: The Chloe sunglasses with rhinestone hearts on the lenses; it was fun for a few months—and only a few months!

FM: Who is film's most fashionable leading man?

SS: I have several: Marcello Mastroianni, Marlon Brando, Sean Penn, Ed Norton, Nicolas Cage. There is a certain type of charisma that links these men, an indefinable blend of strength and vulnerability.

FM: What is your favorite fashion scene from a movie?

SS: In *The Royal Tenenbaums*; the scene with Gwyneth Paltrow in the bathtub. She is able to convey that rare quality in movies, a combination of hyper reality and naturalness in a very unusual scene. She looks both comfortable and dissatisfied with her existence simultaneously, and transformed the bathtub into a cool existential "angsty" hangout.

How to Treat Your Feet to a Home Pedicure

by Essie Weingarten of Essie Cosmetics, Ltd.

Essie Weingarten, founder and president of Essie Cosmetics, is a savvy businesswoman whose keen eye for color and flair for names has made her a beauty industry icon. Her passion for the perfect manicure and pedicure led her to create Essie nail polish, the brand of choice in fine salons and spas internationally, with celebrity fans Barbra Streisand, Madonna, Mischa Barton, and Heidi Klum, to name a few. Essie's cult classic, Bullet Slippers (the pinkest pink with white undertones), may be the most recognizable shade on Earth.

It's important to keep feet clean and well-moisturized; the skin on our feet dries out easily, and even the prettiest backless mules lose their glamour when they show off cracked heels. I believe pedicures are an absolute necessity for attractive feet. They're also relaxing and invigorating. Nothing can come close to a good spa pedicure in a salon, but when it's not possible to get there, home care can keep feet presentable and feeling good anytime. And remember: don't neglect pedicures in wintertime just because your toes don't show. Our feet deserve year-round care. They take abuse every day. They support us and take us all over the world, so they deserve some TLC. Besides, a bright polish can brighten even the grayest days when you get home and slip out of your shoes and socks!

STEP 1: Fill a basin or a footbath with warm—not hot—water and add an effervescent foot soak. If you don't have a professional pedicure product, Epsom salts or bath salts will do. Soak your feet for 10 to 20 minutes to soften calluses, cuticles, and dead skin. If you want to add an invigorating essential oil that also disinfects, eucalyptus or peppermint are both excellent and easily available.

STEP 2: Apply a foot scrub to the feet while they're damp. Massage it into the skin with a firm circular motion, paying special attention to areas of thickened skin on the heels and soles. Gently use pumice to smooth calluses. Then scrub the feet well with a brush or loofah.

STEP 3: Dry the feet with a towel. Make sure to dry well between your toes to prevent athlete's foot. Apply cuticle cream or oil to cuticles and use the towel to gently push cuticles back.

STEP 4: Nip hangnails with a nipper (a small scissor-like tool with a spring handle and fine, thin edge lines), but remove only the dry, jagged edges (non-living tissue). Do not cut cuticles. They protect the nail beds, and cutting them unnecessarily will make them thicken.

STEP 5: If you have thick or overgrown cuticles, apply cuticle oil once feet are dry. Leave on for five minutes, then gently push back the cuticle using moistened cotton wrapped around an orangewood cuticle pusher. If you've noticed any torn areas of the cuticles or have removed hangnails, apply a drop of alcohol or other disinfectant to kill bacteria that could cause an infection.

STEP 6: If you have the time, apply a pedicure mask (a moisturizing facial mask can also be used in a pinch). Apply lavishly to each foot, then wrap the feet in warm, moist cloths (or warm, moist paper towels) and cover with plastic wrap or plastic bags. Leave the mask undisturbed for 10 to 15 minutes. In winter, it's nice to tuck the feet under a heating pad, which will also result in greater absorption of the cream. Next, remove the cloths and use them to wipe off the mask. Rinse the feet lightly and pat dry.

STEP 7: Massage the feet using circular motions all over, pressing with your thumb on the sole at the base of each toe. Massage the lower legs with flat, straight strokes. Yes, it's more fun having someone else do it, but you can massage yourself, and it's important for perking up the circulation and moisturizing the feet. If you tend to have calluses, massage in a moisturizer with AHAs (alpha hydroxy acids) to encourage the sloughing off of dead cells. You can also purchase a reflexology chart in most health food stores or find one online and add this ancient science to your massage. You'll be refreshed and relaxed.

⚠ **"My toenail has turned black!"** Black or green areas on a toenail most likely indicates a common fungus that must be treated by a podiatrist. Ingrown nails should also be dealt with only by a professional.

Q&A

FM: Define "timeless."
EW: In my eyes, two things will always be timeless: the little black dress and the elegant red nail.

FM: Who is film's most fashionable leading lady?
EW: Barbra Streisand is a heroine. She had a great impact on women as far as making them recognize the importance of beautiful hands. And Madonna has been a great innovator. She loves nail polish, so we love her!

FM: What is your favorite fashion scene from a movie?
EW: I think every scene from the 1930s film *The Women* is fabulous. The women are witty and well-dressed, and they love meeting one another at the beauty salon.

Daily Foot Care

- Moisturize your feet every day and rub oil into the cuticles.

- Shaping the nails is best left to professionals, but if you must file them yourself, cut them straight across first, then gently round the corners just slightly.

- For extra-dry skin and calluses, apply an ultra-rich moisturizer before bed and cover with natural cotton socks overnight.

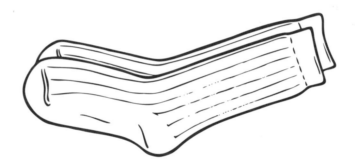

How to Apply Self-Tanner

by Ole Henriksen of Ole Henriksen Face/Body spa

A native of Denmark, Ole (pronounced Oo-la) Henriksen researched skin care treatments in Jakarta, Indonesia, before studying cosmetology in London. He relocated to Los Angeles and opened Ole Henriksen Face/Body in Beverly Hills, where his all-natural skincare inspired early client Barbra Streisand to spread the word to the celebrity set, earning him the nickname "facialist to the stars." Henriksen recently opened One at Shutters on the Beach, and is the author of Ole Henriksen's Seven Day Skin Care Program.

Self tanning is more popular than ever, and understandably so, as it is an easy and safe way to achieve that beautiful golden glow. Celebrity clients of my spa, like Charlize Theron, Ben Stiller, and Debra Messing, are all huge fans of self-tanners. But to ensure a successful self-tanning experience, I recommend patience and always using a high-quality product.

Self-tanner is best applied in the morning. If you take the time to follow each step and perfect your application, you will reduce the chances of a streaky, orange, fake-looking tan.

STEP 1: Choose a self-tanner that is right for your skin color. Self-tanners generally come in light, medium, or dark, with slight variations from brand to brand. You may have to experiment with a few different brands to find the right shade for your skin. In my experience, self-tanning products are strictly for fair-to light-olive-pigmented skin. Olive skin with dark pigment and black skin do best with an oil-based hydrating body lotion that adds luminosity to skin color rather than self-tanning products. People with fair skin should purchase the lightest shade of self-tanners, while those with light olive skin (or a fair black complexion) should settle for a medium shade so the self-tanner will look natural. Dark self-tanners tend to look like they are painted on.

STEP 2: Apply a body scrub, massaged into the entire body in firm, circular motions. The key to a successful tan application is the preparatory skin conditioning. Completely smooth and soft body skin is required for the self-tanner to glide on evenly and bind with the skin's surface layer. Wet the body, turn the shower off, and begin the process, working from the feet upward on each leg, covering every square inch of body tissue. An ideal body scrub should contain enough humectants (hydrators) that body tissue does not dry out after the scrub. The skin should be retexturized yet moist, without a greasy mantle. Let the skin dry naturally with a terrycloth robe wrapped around the body.

STEP 3: Apply. Do not squeeze the self-tanner directly onto your skin—you'll risk an uneven application. Instead, blend the tanner between the palms of your hands and then massage it into your skin in long, firm, circular motions. As with the scrub, the best place to start are the feet and legs, working your way steadily upward. (If you are going for complete body coverage, you will need some help with the back area.) Massage with your entire palms for an even application. Use enough self-tanner on each section of the skin for an even glide across the entire body so that one application will do the job and the tan will look natural. You don't need to worry about specific areas like knees, ankles, or elbows—as long as you keep applying in firm circular motions, even these trickier areas should be fine.

Self tanners on the face are very tricky; they often settle into the pores and make pores look bigger. For faces, I strictly recommend a tinted moisturizer for a tanned look.

STEP 4: Let the self-tanner absorb for 15 to 25 minutes before you put your clothes back on. Use a scrub brush to vigorously scrub your palms free of self-tanner, but leave the tanner on the tops of your hands.

STEP 5: Apply body lotion a couple of hours later to enhance the golden sheen.

⚠ **"My self-tan is streaky."** If you find that streaking has occurred (you won't know until the tan develops), you can try to remove the self-tanner by scrubbing the trouble area with rubbing alcohol and a terry face cloth. Apply a thin coat of body lotion to moisturize the area—it will be very dry from the alcohol—and reapply the self-tanner as described above.

Q&A

FM: What's the best style tip you ever got, and from whom?
OH: David Bowie told me years ago, and I live by this, to always dress classically elegant with just a touch of modern trend.

FM: Define "timeless."
OH: Flawless skin.

FM: What's the worst fashion faux pas?
OH: Unbuttoning one button too many on your shirt, with lots of gold chains underneath.

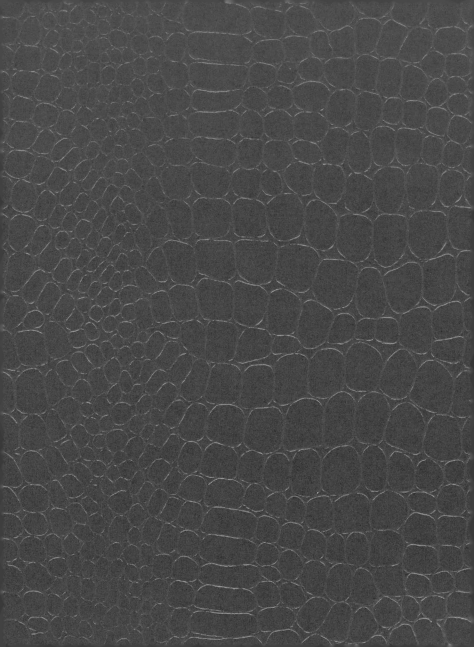

PART TWO

FASHION

How to Find the Perfect Little Black Dress

by Mark Gill of MG Worldwide Inc.

St. Louis native Mark Gill studied business management and opera before realizing his ultimate calling: A year after landing a job at Banana Republic, Gill was named "top contributor," and then "top in worldwide sales" a year later. Gill became a sales consultant for Jil Sander, started his own handbag collection, and began producing fashion shows to showcase international and local designers. Today Gill has his own image consulting company, MG Worldwide Inc., working with clients to constantly enhance their personal image.

To understand the imperative of the little black dress, we must turn to the scene in *Breakfast at Tiffany's*, when Audrey Hepburn's Holly Golightly emerges from the bathroom dressed for her weekly to visit to Sally Tomato in Sing Sing. Although Hepburn wears other black dresses in the film, the clean design of her slim sleeveless outfit is still fresh and modern after more than forty years.

But as perfect as that iconic dress was for her, it's not the right silhouette for every woman. In my style seminars, I bring in a similar dress (a slim, sleeveless, back-zipped shift with a boat neck), and typically only 2 out of every 10 women are able to wear it. Every woman needs to know how to find a dress that matches her particular body type. In this case, let's work from the classic *Breakfast at Tiffany's* model: a structured black dress that can go from day to night and lend itself as a canvas to accessories.

STEP 1: Identify your body type. In order to get a little black dress that works for your body and your wardrobe, you have to understand what looks good on you—a deceptively simple task. To do this, take a good look at your body and match it to one of these four basic silhouettes:

- **Rectangular:** You are shaped a little like a boy, with a longer torso that goes right into your hips. This shape—in which the torso and hips are often in a straight line—is usually accompanied by a broader shoulder and a slightly flat chest.

  Solution: You need to create the illusion of curves by picking a dress with a slightly empire shape. Look for details like a line (piping or stitching) about three inches (7.5 cm) under the bust. This will give you a waistline where there is none and naturally enhance your bust.

- **Hourglass:** You are a voluptuous woman, with a bigger chest, an indented waist, and a noticeable curve to your hips.

  Solution: You will look best in an A-line dress that "grabs" your waist and flows out over your hips, accompanied by a fitted top with darts and a V-neck, which is particularly flattering to a larger bust line.

- **Top heavy:** You have wider shoulders and larger breasts with a torso that tapers down to an indented waist, slim hips, and thin legs.

  Solution: Look for a dress with a draped (perhaps even slightly blouson) top and fitted skirt that "grabs" you where you are slimmest: the lower half of your body.

- **Bottom heavy:** You have wide hips and a slim torso, the opposite of "top heavy," above.

  Solution: Your shape will be enhanced by a fitted top and straight skirt that is wider at the hip and falls straight (a "pipe" shape), unlike a pencil skirt that tapers at the knee.

STEP 2: Accessorize your dress to go from the office to a nighttime function. For junior executives and assistants, an appropriate daytime/work look is a cardigan over your dress (with the sleeves pushed up to make it interesting), diamond stud earrings (or a reasonable facsimile), and some pearls. Then funk it up at night by adding a black tight and a riding or stretch leather fitted boot with slender high heel. Tuck a lightweight turtleneck under your dress, or throw a cable knit sweater or leather jacket over it.

For those in an executive or "boardroom" position, create a daytime look by adding a blazer—but not a boxy, "eighties" power version. You want a little cropped blazer with a notched-collar jacket and a one-button closure to accent the waist and maybe three-quarter sleeves for a casual look. At night, tie a scarf around your throat and tuck it into the neckline of the dress. Add a pair of sling backs, a little clutch, and throw a cardigan over your shoulders.

⚠ **"Help! I love the concept, but I look awful in black."** Sometimes your little black dress problem is not a body issue—it's a complexion issue. First, try a dress with a scoop or V-neck that will keep the solid black fabric from being so close to your face. If that doesn't work, then simply don't wear black; instead, accessorize with it. Dress yourself in pink, chartreuse, periwinkle, or bone, and add a black patent leather belt. Pop on a pair of patent sling backs; carry a slim black patent clutch. For a jazzier nighttime look, forgo the pearls and add a beaded black choker.

Q&A

FM: What's the best style tip you ever got, and from whom?
MG: It wasn't a tip; it was a lesson. The first time I saw Miuccia Prada send a floral-printed short-sleeve dress paired with motorcycle boots down the runaway, I thought, "Genius." That's a look for a woman who doesn't want to be a lady who lunches, and I love working with that girl.

FM: Define "fashion forward."
MG: Mixing the high with the low—the "label" with the everyday basic, like a beaded top with blue jeans—makes fashion unpredictable.

FM: What's your favorite fashion scene from a movie?
MG: Cate Blanchett costumed in *Elizabeth*: I the love the medieval period for its graceful and dark elegance.

Choosing the Best Material

Don't get fooled into buying a black dress made from matte jersey. Although that fabric is fluid and stretches for comfort (great for exercise pants), keep a mental picture of Hepburn's architectural little black dress in mind and settle on a soft wool gabardine with a touch of Lycra that will hold its shape—as well as yours.

For women with a more challenging body type, the best little black dress will be unstructured and of a fabric that does not drape (which means *without Lycra*). The shape of this dress should be accented with individualized tailoring details, according to each woman's body shape.

How to Buy a Contemporary White Blouse

by Nick Wheeler of Charles Tyrwhitt Shirts

Nick Wheeler (full name Nicholas Charles Tyrwhitt Wheeler) founded Charles Tyrwhitt Shirts in November 1986, with the aim of filling the gap between average, everyday British shirt makers and high-end formal shirt tailors like Turnbull & Asser. His mail-order operation may have sent out its early orders in brown jiffy bags, but today Charles Tyrwhitt is one of the foremost suppliers of formal shirts in England, with a vast clientele around the globe and retail stores in London, Paris, and New York.

The crisp, pure white blouse is a wardrobe staple because it matches anything and everything. It can be basic or fashionable, classic or jazzy. It will suit any complexion and instantly makes the wearer look fresh and stylish. Depending on its fit and fabric, the right white blouse can top off a pair of jeans, tailored trousers, or even become part of an evening look. (Let's not forget Sharon Stone wearing her husband's tailored white shirt with a lavender ball skirt at the 1998 Oscars.) A white blouse is the perfect frame for your most exciting jewelry. But before you even start thinking of all the ways you can wear a white blouse, you have to concentrate on fit: That's the most important aspect.

STEP 1: Choose the right shape for your style. There are three basic blouse shapes:

- **Classic:** The classic shirt is nonfitted, meaning that it does not have darts, and as a result, it does not taper into the body. Fabric possibilities for the nonfitted shirt are cotton or fine linen, with long or short sleeves, but the generous fit makes this shirt slightly bulky to tuck in.
- **Tailored:** The tailored shirt is semifitted, with front, back, and bust-line darts, creating a slightly slimmer body silhouette. This blouse works well

in silk or Sea Island–quality cotton (a particularly fine fabric, made with long, silky fibers), with long or three-quarter length sleeves.

- **Fitted:** This is the slimmest version, with darts beside the bust and along the length of the back. This blouse should be made from a stretch-cotton fabric to give a comfortable yet elegant figure-skimming shape. It can have long sleeves or be sleeveless.

STEP 2: Consider the quality of the shirt.

- The placket (the opening in the front of the blouse where the button-holes are located) should be made from double layers of fabric, with material between the layers to provide support and strength.
- There should not be any inconsistent stiching or loose threads.
- Buttons should be pearlised plastic or, even better, center-cut mother-of-pearl, which is made from the hard, smooth, iridescent inner lining of the shells of oysters, mussels, and other mollusks. You can determine if a button is mother-of-pearl by tapping it against your teeth. Mother-of-pearl should feel hard and make a clean sound. Plastic will sound dull when tapped against the teeth.
- The buttonholes should be clean, without loose threads, and the buttons should be sewn on with cross-stitching for extra strength.

STEP 3: Try on the shirt, keeping the following details in mind:

- The shoulder seam should line up with the top of your natural shoulder, and the bottom seam should attach to the armhole smoothly and evenly.
- When the shirt is buttoned, the placket should not pucker or pull, particularly across the center of the bust. The darts should match the contours of the body (for example, the point of a bust-line dart should fall below the center of the breast, not above or at the center) and should also lay flat without puckering.
- If the sleeve length and cuff fit correctly, you should be able to extend your arm in any direction without the cuff pulling away from the wrist.

- Check the seams on the sides of the body of the shirt. Whether single or double stitched, side seams should never twist in toward your stomach or twist away toward your back. If they do, the blouse will never keep its shape after laundering.

STEP 4: Pay special attention to the shirt's collar. Think of the face as a picture and the collar of the blouse as a frame. The length and spread of the collar points should complement the head's contour and size. The collar button should close without pulling on the neck; this will ensure it sits correctly when worn undone.

Q&A

FM: What's the best style tip you ever got, and from whom?
NW: It's better to be underdressed than over dressed, from my wife.

FM: Who is your favorite style icon?
NW: Cary Grant—he took the English look and sold it to the world.

FM: What is your favorite fashion scene from a movie?
NW: Sean Connery as James Bond in the film *Goldfinger*, wearing his dinner jacket, driving his Aston Martin DB5, and luring Pussy Galore. It sets the tone for the swinging '60s.

How to Choose the Perfect T-Shirt

by Pauline Sokol Nakios of Lilla P

Inspired by the desire to find the perfect T, Pauline Sokol Nakios founded Lilla P, named after her late grandmother. Guided by core principles of simplicity, quality, and value, Nakios focuses on classic designs in luxurious fabrics and enticing colors to offer a full line of basics as well as contemporary shapes. Her T-shirts are sold in better stores throughout the United States and the Caribbean.

If there's one sure way to build variation into your wardrobe today, it's with T-shirts. In a way, the T-shirt is like the contemporary version of the blouse—just as much of a fashion staple, but easier to wear and more versatile. T-shirts present a great opportunity to experiment with color, and their reasonable cost makes it painless to replenish your selections each season. The various fabric contents and textures used today also work to create new silhouettes—from the classic shape to the cut of the moment, T-shirts have serious fashion flexibility. Wear a brightly colored T-shirt under a dark jacket or sweater and you have a fresh look. To find a T-shirt that will flatter your body, consider the following.

NECKLINE. Find the best neckline for your body type. Generally speaking:

- **Chesty:** Try a deep V-neck or scoop that takes your eye down. Avoid high necklines, which draw the eye up and make your breasts look as if they are hanging too low.
- **Small Chest:** Enhance a smaller chest with lines that draw the eye up or across, like jewel and boat necks.
- **Broad Shoulders:** Wear necklines that sit close to the neck and do not extend too far out toward the shoulder to draw the eye into the neck. Don't wear boat necks, which will accentuate the width of the shoulders.

- **Short Neck:** Plunging necklines (a deep V-neck) or open necklines (boat neck or scoop neck) will elongate the neck. Stay away from turtlenecks and high necklines that make the neck appear shorter.

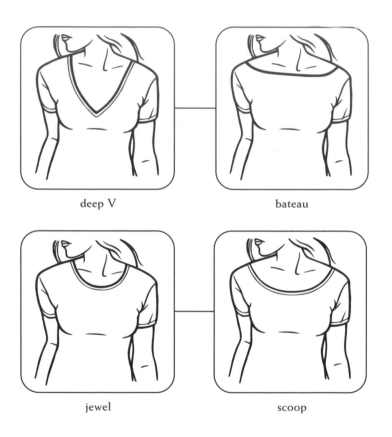

deep V

bateau

jewel

scoop

LENGTH. Season by season, fashion takes us from long to short, and layering with varying lengths can be fun. But the best wardrobe building block is a

T-shirt that hits right at or just below the hip, a very flattering proportion for almost everyone. Side vents can be a nice finishing touch and make it possible to wear the shirt untucked without looking sloppy. If a shirt is too long, it will make your legs and lower body look shorter. Keep in mind that trendy styles are not always the most flattering.

SLEEVES. Although sleeve length is a personal preference, there is an age when many women no longer feel comfortable exposing their arms. The three-quarter length sleeve is probably the most universally flattering. A short sleeve can be tricky. Somewhere between the cap and the short sleeve is best—if it's too long, the sleeve can square you off and make you look blocky. If you have good arms, by all means, show them off by wearing tanks. I have found that tanks with cut-in shoulders are the most flattering—especially for those with broader shoulders. Always make sure that the tank covers that little pocket of fat that many of us have right under the armhole area—when you find one, buy it in every color!

FIT. A T-shirt should be fitted, but not so much that it reveals what you want to hide (bra fat is a major concern for many women). This doesn't always mean adding Lycra—I prefer an all-cotton shirt that drapes nicely against the body. A skin-tight tee will find flaws in even the most perfect body

FABRIC AND COLOR. Since layering T-shirts is a good way to play with color in your wardrobe, choose a lighter weight fabric that doesn't add bulk. Although it is trendy to layer offbeat color combinations (like purple over Kelly green), you can also go tone on tone (like brown over black) for a more classic look.

FM: What's the worst fashion faux pas?
PSN: Wearing cargo pants with stilettos.

FM: Define "fashion forward."
PSN: Classic with a twist; clean lines with one element of the season—but never more than one at a time.

FM: Who's film's most fashionable leading man?
PSN: James Dean—he gave T-shirts such cachet.

EXTRA HELP

What Lies Beneath

Lacy underpinnings don't work well with T-shirts, and regardless of skin tone, your best bra color is nude, not white. A nude colored, smooth contoured bra is the best investment you can make.

How to Buy and Care for Cashmere

by Christopher Fischer of C3 Concepts

With more than 25 years of experience in the knitwear industry, British-born Christopher Fischer is one of the leading authorities in cashmere design and manufacturing technology. His company's headquarters in midtown Manhattan is home to a showroom and international design studio. Christopher Fischer cashmere collections are sold in their own stores and the very best retail and department stores around the world, including Bergdorf Goodman, Barneys New York, Saks Fifth Avenue, Neiman Marcus, Fred Segal, and Henri Bendel.

The name cashmere ("the fiber of kings") comes from Kashmir, the mountainous area of India and Pakistan, but the fiber itself actually came from Tibet. Cashmere's use as a luxury fiber can be dated as far back as Roman times and perhaps even before—legend has it that the Arc of the Covenant of the Old Testament was lined with woven cashmere fabric. In more recent times, it was popularized by the Empress Eugenie, wife of Napoleon III. She had the fiber woven in France into her famous "ring shawl," so called because it could be drawn through her wedding ring.

But not all cashmere is created equal. Where it comes from, how it is graded and sorted, and the way it is dyed all play a part in determining the characteristics of the fiber, but the best fibers actually come from Inner Mongolia or China.

PURCHASE

STEP 1: Let your fingers, not the price tag, tell you about the quality. Although cashmere is expensive, don't be misled into thinking a sweater is high quality because of a high price. It is certainly not always true that a higher cost is indicative of better quality. Touch the sweater—it should feel soft and luxe, not scratchy and "brittle" like a wool. Generally, the sweater should have a soft and slightly spongy "top" surface, not too fuzzy or matted, with defined stitch clarity.

STEP 2: Examine the clarity of the color. No matter the color, the hue of the sweater should be bright, vibrant, clear, and clean, with depth and saturation in even the darker colors and black: certainly not grayish, dull, faded, or dirty looking.

STEP 3: Look at the seams. Top-quality sweaters are usually fully fashioned, meaning the panels of the garment are all knit exactly to shape and size, giving it the cleanest and neatest finish possible on all the seams. No seams are cut and then sewn together—the knitted panels are linked together by hand with cashmere yarn, stitch by stitch. All visible seams are then finished by hand for a "seamless" look. If there are buttons, each should also be sewn on with cashmere yarn, not cotton thread.

STEP 4: Examine the yarn itself. All cashmere knitting yarn is first spun into single-ply yarn. Then two ends of the single plies are twisted together into a 2-ply yarn, which makes the yarn more stable. Knitting a single-ply yarn would cause the garment to twist and torque. (I am sure you have had T-shirts on which the side seams start twisting to the front and the back.)

For quality garments, the yarn is always 2-ply. Using multiple plies of 2-ply yarns to get a 6-ply, 8-ply, or 10-ply does not improve the quality of the garment; it just makes it heavier and more expensive.

CARE

STEP 1: Always take care when putting on, or taking off, your sweater. Because cashmere is so soft, be careful not to overstretch the neck opening or any delicate seam, which could cause the yarn to break.

STEP 2: All cashmere sweaters will pill, even those made from the very best quality fiber. Pilling is caused by loose and shorter cashmere hairs coming out of the surface through natural friction during wear and abrading together to form little hairballs.

To keep the sweater's best appearance, just pull these off by hand after every wear. You can also use a very soft bristle lint brush, but always brush downward, in the direction of the knitting stitches, and lightly.

Cashmere has become a very fashionable item, and today's most fashionable knits feature light and loose textures. But this looseness and lighter weight causes the sweaters to be much more delicate and fragile. They will pill more, and so fashion comes at a price.

STEP 3: Always hand wash or dry-clean cashmere.
FOR HAND WASHING:

- Wash each garment separately in cool, tepid water. Use only a small amount of high quality mild shampoo. Do not use any bleach or harsh detergents, which will remove all the natural oils in the fibers and cause the garment to feel harsh and brittle.
- Gently squeeze the garment in the soapy water. Do not rub. Wash quickly. Do not let the garment soak. Rinse repeatedly in cool water until the water is clean and clear of any soap. Gently squeeze out any excess water. Do not wring the garment.
- Put the garment into a wash bag or pillow case and spin out any remaining excess water using the spin cycle on your washing machine. You can also place the sweater flat on a clean dry towel and roll it up, applying pressure to squeeze out any excess water.
- To dry, place the sweater flat on another clean, dry towel, pulling the garment into shape. Make sure all the ribs and cuffs are closed and tight together, not stretched open. Dry in an airy place away from direct sun-

light and away from radiators or any direct heat. Once thoroughly dry, the garment can be delicately tumbled in a home dryer at a cool temperature (air dry, no heat) to make the fibers "bloom." Put the garment inside-out in a lingerie bag or pillow case, then tumble for a short time.

- When dry, pick off any pills or yarn balls. Gently steam the garment to shape. Steam through the sweater to lift the top surface—do not directly iron and press the sweater, which could scorch the surface. To be safe, use a clean damp cloth over the sweater when you steam. Leave in an airy place to dry and cool. Fold flat and store. Do not hang.

FOR DRY CLEANING:

- Ensure that the dry cleaner is experienced in cleaning cashmere.
- Always tell your dry cleaner that the garment is cashmere.
- Advise your dry cleaner of your preferred chest and length measurements, so that they can block the garment to your correct size.

STEP 4: If you are storing your sweater for any length of time, first wash or dry clean the garment, then fold and wrap it with acid-free tissue paper. Do not store the sweater in a sealed plastic bag, as the sweater will not be able to breathe.

Q&A

FM: Define "timeless."
CF: A white-faced, stainless steel Rolex Daytona watch.

FM: What's the best style tip you ever got, and from whom?
CF: Always have clean and polished shoes, from my prep school housemaster.

FM: Who's your favorite style icon?
CF: My father: He had his own individual style, and he would never think to follow anyone else.

Cashmere Facts

The quality of raw cashmere fiber is determined by the length of the hair, the fineness of the hair, and the whiteness of the color (with the longest, finest, and whitest fiber being the most expensive). If a sweater is made from shorter length fiber, the surface will pill more, and the fibers will shed and separate from the knitted sweater more easily. If you use coarser fiber, it will not feel as soft and will instead feel more "scratchy and itchy."

Cashmere hair comes in a range of natural colors, from pure white to natural browns and almost black. Using pure white fiber will achieve the brightest, clearest, and cleanest looking colors, while non-white grades will produce grayed, dull, and "dirty" looking colors.

The expense of cashmere, no matter its use, is simply a matter of supply and demand: Each Capra Hirus goat (not a breed, but a specific type of goat that is the source of cashmere fiber, raised principally in China, Mongolia, Afghanistan, Iran, India, and Pakistan) produces only about 4 ounces of fine cashmere fiber in a year (at the very most), and it takes two or three years (at the very least) for a goat to produce enough cashmere for a small ladies' sweater. High quality raw cashmere fiber can be so fine that there may be more than 7 miles of fiber in a classic twin set!

How to Buy a Bra That Fits

by Michael Rabinowitz of Le Mystère

Le Mystère founder and CEO Michael Rabinowitz began his career in the intimate apparel industry more than 30 years ago. His established expertise has fulfilled Le Mystère's mission statement, providing comfortable products, excellent fit, excellent service, and excellent delivery. South-African born Rabinowitz's belief that lingerie must anticipate fashion needs accounts for the wide range of Le Mystère's line (including the famous molded Tisha T-shirt bra). The company counts many famous Hollywood stars among its fans.

Building a good wardrobe means dressing properly from the inside out, and the correct bra size is key. Wearing a bra that fits correctly affects posture as well as the health of breast tissue (if the bra is too loose, the breast tissue sags; if it's too tight, the underwire can poke you in your most sensitive areas)—not to mention, breasts without the proper support can make you look heavier and older.

Since Le Mystere's slogan is "It's All About Fit," we have a pretty good handle on getting the best fit for each woman. But every woman's frame and shape is different, and it can be a bit tricky to measure yourself. Would it surprise you to know that most women are actually wearing the incorrect size?

Your bra size can change for many reasons (from weight fluctuations to brand variations), so get regular fittings and replace your bras: every six months is ideal, every year is a must.

STEP 1: Determine your band size. While you are wearing your own bra, use a measuring tape to measure around the rib cage (just beneath the breasts), keeping the tape straight and snug around the back. If you measure an even number, add 4 inches to your measurement for your band size. If you measure an odd number, add 5 inches to attain your band size.

For example: Measuring 32 inches around the rib cage means the calculation is:

> **32 INCHES + 4 INCHES = 36 INCHES**

Measuring 31 inches around the rib cage means the calculation is:

> **31 INCHES + 5 INCHES = 36 INCHES.**

Fuller figured women, please note: If you measure more than 36 inches around your rib cage, you may need to add only 1 to 3 inches in order to get to the next even-numbered band size. If your rib cage measures 38 to 44 inches, you do not need to add any additional length.

STEP 2: Determine your cup size. Measure around the fullest part of the bust, keeping the tape straight and snug. Subtract this measurement from your rib cage measurement. That number is now the basis for your cup size. Cup size in the United States is calculated on an ascending numerical scale starting at 1 inch for an "A" cup. For every inch of difference, you go to the next cup size.

For example: If the measurement around the fullest part of your breasts is 40 inches and your rib cage measurement is 36 inches, that means 4 inches is your cup size. Determine the corresponding letter size according to the following scale:

1 inch	A cup
2 inches	B cup
3 inches	C cup
4 inches	D cup
5 inches	DD cup (E)
6 inches	DDD cup (F)
7 inches	DDDD cup (G)

STEP 3: Put the bra on properly. Never put on a bra by hooking it underneath your breasts and spinning it around so the closure is in the back. Instead, lean forward into the cups, lacing your breasts into the supports and reaching behind to hook the bra on the middle hooks of the closure.

STEP 4: Adjust the straps. If the straps cut deeply into the skin, find a bra with a thicker shoulder strap or a strap with a thin layer of padding or gel for comfort. Make sure to adjust the straps every time you put on a bra.

STEP 5: Now, determine the bra's fit:

- Make sure your breast fills the cup completely, without spilling over the top. A bra is too small when you put on a shirt and see a "bump" where the breast meets the top line of the cup.
- If the cups of the bra are wrinkly, lift your breast and place it correctly into the cup. If, after you readjust the cup, it is still wrinkly, the cup is probably too large. If your breasts bunch up on the sides, the cup is probably too small.
- Make sure that there is a plush covering on underwires for maximum comfort.
- The small piece of fabric suspended between the cups should lay flat against your breastbone.

BAND SIZE CONVERSION		
US/UK	**EUROPEAN**	**FRENCH**
32	70	85
34	75	90
36	80	95
38	85	100
40	90	105
42	95	110
44	100	115

⚠ **"My undergarments seem to age easily."** Lingerie is the closest thing to your skin and requires extra care to keep in perfect shape. You will get the best results by hand washing your bras in lukewarm water with a gentle care product. Squeeze—never wring—the water out and always line-dry. Never use bleach and never expose lingerie to dryer heat: Both cause shrinkage and damage the elasticity, which affects fit.

Q&A

FM: Who is film's most fashionable leading lady?
MR: Audrey Hepburn, because, even though petite, she knew how to carry herself.

FM: Who is your favorite style icon?
MR: Madonna.

FM: What is your favorite fashion scene from a movie?
MR: *My Fair Lady*, because the women looked so good in their magnificent hats, especially in the scene at the Ascot races.

How to Learn to Love Your Thong

by Gale Epstein of Hanky Panky

Gale Epstein is the president and creative director of Hanky Panky, a company she founded with her friend Lida Orzeck after designing embroidered handkerchief lingerie for her as a gift. Epstein's lingerie and sleepwear designs, available in boutiques and specialty stores, have been featured in Elle, In Style, Marie-Claire, Oprah, *and the* New Yorker. *The* Wall Street Journal *also did a front-page story on the cult status of Epstein's most famous garment, the #4811 thong. Hanky Panky sells more than three million thongs a year.*

Somewhere between the G-string and the panty brief falls the thong. For devotees, there is no turning back: The only underwear they'll ever wear is a thong. But others have not yet been converted, primarily because they imagine themselves pulling improperly fitting panties from their nether regions.

And there you have it—the biggest obstacle to wearing a thong is not below the waist but above it: Many women just can't accept the fact that a thong can be sexy and comfortable. The truth is that the right thong can be more comfortable than any other panty, and it will rid you of panty lines (especially important in this day of Lycra everything). Beautiful and efficient: You just have to know what to look for in a thong and what to expect.

STEP 1: Face your fears. Many women have a mental block against the thong because they fret about the way they are going to look in one. Somehow, you have to get beyond that. If you judge the appropriateness of any garment you wear by backing into a mirror in a brightly lit room to examine every square inch of your posterior, you probably won't have a stitch in your wardrobe. Why hold yourself up to that kind of scrutiny? Treat yourself with a little more kindness, and get beyond the judgment stage and into the comfort zone.

STEP 2: Look for a thong made from the softest, most comfortable fabric. I prefer stretchable lace because it is extremely forgiving, which means it adapts to a wide variety of body shapes and sizes and moves with you. Pick the thong up and drape it over your hand: It should be pliable and extremely light (our bestselling model weighs only half an ounce, the same as about four cloves of garlic) and every part of it should feel soft to the touch, particularly any decorative detail or stitching.

Pay special attention to the edges of the thong. I recommend a thin line of soft stretchable lace instead of an elastic band. It has just the right amount of modulus, or elasticity, to stretch against the skin, ensuring a good fit without binding and eventually chafing.

STEP 3: The secret of the thong is to find a gusset that fits. The gusset (or crotch lining) of the thong must be cotton—that much everyone knows. But did you know that everything revolves around that piece of fabric? It is critical

to fit. The gusset of a thong can't be too short back to front (or you know exactly what will happen). But it also cannot be too narrow from side to side.

If there's a secret to comfort in wearing a thong, that's it. The gusset must be wide enough (and soft enough, yet not too bulky) to lay flat against the body when stretched and not roll in on the sides, causing an uncomfortable ridge in your most sensitive body area.

STEP 4: Buy one, wash it, and wear it. If there are areas of discomfort, you will have to determine whether it is the style of that particular thong and, if so, use the problem areas as a guide on the next trial purchase. But if you have followed these steps, there is every chance that you will wind up with a sexy and comfortable undergarment that eliminates panty lines and, under it all, bestows a sense of liberation.

Q&A

FM: Who is film's most fashionable leading lady?
GE: That would be Lassie, because she wears her fabulous fur coat unselfconsciously.

FM: Who is film's most fashionable leading man?
GE: King Kong, ditto.

FM: What's your favorite fashion scene from a movie?
GE: In the 1957 movie *Funny Face*, Kay Thompson's gray-and-white clad character (playing Diana Vreeland) bursts upon the Technicolor scene through pink doors with the Declaration of Pink Dependence. Besides pink prescience, the scene is packed with fashion "blood, brains, and 'bazzazz.'"

How to Match Your Hosiery to Your Wardrobe

by Arden Hess of Wolford

Fashion expert Arden Hess is the spokesperson for the luxurious "World of Wolford," a preeminent maker of luxury leg and body wear. Founded on the shores of Lake Constance in Austria in 1949 by pioneers Reinhold Wolff and Walter Palmers, Wolford has established itself worldwide as a luxury name for hosiery, body wear, swimwear, and underwear.

The old adage about starting at the bottom takes on new meaning when you think about getting dressed from the toes up. In one minute, a simple pair of tights can update any ensemble, giving you a much more polished look. Hosiery can be used to tie everything together in your wardrobe as well as add comfort and warmth. When covered by quality hosiery, your feet are better supported in your shoes, and sensitive skin is protected by soft fibers. Hosiery can also make your legs look slimmer and more beautiful. The right pair of tights seduces, conceals, tans, and bestows elegance.

But don't limit yourself to thinking everything has to "match" and be the same exact hue as your clothing. There are just so many colors and textures to choose from. For me, it's fun to try textures and contrast colors to create interesting combinations. Two basic techniques will guide you through the case studies that follow:

- **For a classic look,** coordinate your hosiery with your shoe color and your clothing's texture. For example, if you're wearing a gray skirt with black shoes, your hosiery should be in same color family as the shoe instead of "matching" the hem: in other words, black. But not just any black. Assess the texture of your skirt: A gray skirt in a heavier material and sporty shoes can stand up to textured and patterned knits. But if your skirt is a silvery gray taffeta and your shoes are a delicate black satin, you need the sheerest hosiery in the black hue family.

- **For an adventurous look,** expand your personal style with harmonizing styles and textures. Instead of staying within the range of the same hue, think about hosiery in harmonizing colors (working in tones, like cool shades in the blue/green family, or warm, in the red/orange) and textures. If you are wearing all black, find interesting black textures. If you are wild about wearing red, try shades of pink that work well with it; if you have a lot of brown in your wardrobe, freshen it up by wearing orange. With a little practice, you will gain confidence and know what looks best on you.

CASE 1: YOU'RE WEARING NEUTRALS.

What matches neutrals? More neutrals. Mix gray and brown, navy and black, ivory and brown, and so forth. If you are wearing a bone-colored wool skirt and brown suede chunky loafers, brown ribbed tights are perfect.

For a more adventurous look, add just one brighter tone or color: If you are wearing a navy A-line with navy flats, try fuchsia hosiery instead of the predictable navy.

CASE 2: IT'S COLD OUTSIDE.

Dress your legs in Merino tights as long as the weight of the wool is thin and elegant but not bulky. The right lightweight wool tights can be very refined and versatile; they'll even work under pants. If you're wearing skirts in colder months, adding lightweight Merino tights in the same color as your boots (especially if you are wearing a shorter skirt) can help lengthen the look of your legs.

CASE 3: YOU'RE WEARING A BLACK DRESS.

This is your opportunity to go crazy! Gorgeous black lace hosiery will perk up any dress, but you can also try a colored tight in a brighter tone for a more festive occasion. Colored sheers will provide a more subtle take, and fishnets in colors are always great for spicing up the simple black dress. Any interesting hosiery will start a conversation at a party. Even a simple seam up the back of the leg will get people talking and asking where you got them.

CASE 4: YOU'RE WEARING MULTICOLORED SHOES.

Select one color of the shoe you want to match and remember the colors in the rest of your outfit. If your suede shoe has a brown base with red and yellow accents, you might wear red tights with a basically brown outfit or visa versa. Use the style of your shoe (whether it's sporty or elegant) as a guide to the look you are striving for. A chunky shoe with a thick sole can stand up to a thicker opaque tight. For a slim pump, choose a sheer or a thinner opaque.

⚠ **"How do I care for hosiery to make them last longer?"** Sadly, there is no secret to longer life aside from being very careful not to snag your hosiery and taking care to wash and dry them properly. I recommend washing your hosiery (even sheers) in the washing machine on a gentle cycle in a small load.

Place the hosiery in a soft mesh bag to keep them from catching on anything else in your washing machine, and allow the hose to air-dry. Never put hosiery in the dryer: The high heat can break down fibers. (Fortunately, hosiery dries quickly so you don't have to deal with things hanging all over your bathroom for days.)

FM: What is the worst fashion faux pas?

KH: Wearing knee-highs with a skirt when you really need tights: When you sit down, the skirt reveals your little secret, and unless you are a teenager or a trendsetter, it's not too cute.

FM: Who is film's most fashionable leading man?

KH: Cary Grant. I'm a sucker for the classics, and it's ruined me. I thought I would grow up with cabarets, dinner and dancing, and Fred Astaire to save the day.

FM: What's your favorite fashion scene from a movie?

KH: *All About Eve*, when they are getting ready and having the cocktail party. Bette Davis is all glam, wearing that big brooch, and Marilyn Monroe looks demure—everyone is so elegant, the way I wish it could be today.

EXTRA HELP

How Do I Choose Between Sheers and Opaques?

- Sheers come in hose of varying thickness, which we call denier. The sheerest is a 5 denier, best for a dressy night look. The thickest becomes "opaque," which is harder to see through and goes up to a very thick 80 denier. Opaque 50 denier hose are versatile for both day and night.

- Both sheer and opaque hose are available in matte or shiny finishes and are available in neutrals or colors that change each season. Keep in mind that opaque tights are more slimming.

HOW TO SPOT A COMFORTABLE AND SEXY SHOE

by Donald J Pliner of the Donald J Pliner Collection

Chicago native Donald J Pliner was born with a silver shoehorn in hand, learning the tricks of the trade in his family-operated Florsheim Family Shoe Stores. After his early success with Pappagallo and the Right Bank Clothing Company and Right Bank Shoe Company, Pliner debuted his own line of shoes in 1989. Today the Donald J Pliner Collection features luxury comfort footwear and accessories for women and men (and dogs!), available in Pliner's boutiques, department stores, and better specialty stores.

Do you know the old wives' tale that a comfortable shoe can't be sexy and a sexy shoe can't be comfortable? Well, it isn't true. Shoemaking is about anatomy, and when a shoe designer understands the foot and its complex connection to the rest of the body, you can get both. I know that making comfortable and sexy shoes is possible because I do it every day. But depending on me to make the right shoe is only half of the equation; you must also know how to shop for it.

The individual features of a shoe—straps, bows, and other decoration—are a product of design and a matter of taste. However, good fit is not open to interpretation; shoes must fit in very specific ways to provide your body with support, balance, and mobility. When your shoes are uncomfortable, so is the body and the mind—and that is never sexy.

STEP 1: When choosing a shoe to try on, be realistic about matching the height of the heel to your fashion intentions. If you think a stiletto wears with the same ease as a loafer, it pays to remember that the body isn't built for high heels. The anatomy of the foot is designed for motion, and anything more than a 2¹/₂-inch (6 cm) heel creates abnormal pressure in the front of the foot and instability at the ankle, making the wear less comfortable.

STEP 2: Choose a shoe with a vamp that provides the right amount of support in relation the height of the heel. The vamp is the front line on the top of the shoe, covering the instep. The higher the vamp, the more the support, and the more likely your foot will be "held" in the right position (with the ball over the widest part of the sole).

If you choose too low a vamp (to reveal "toe cleavage"), you remove that support, especially when you are wearing high heels, which already angle the feet forward. As you walk, your foot will slide back and forth, rubbing against the upper lining of the shoe, and you will develop corns. (Look at the feet of someone who wears cowboy boots and you'll rarely see corns. That's because the vamp, from which the shaft of the boot extends, keeps the foot from sliding forward.)

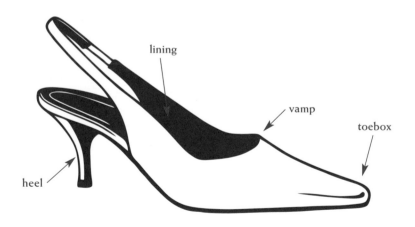

STEP 3: Keep in mind that there is no such thing as exact sizing. Every single shoe that a manufacturer produces—regardless of style—is built upon a "last": a model of a foot that is used to supply anatomical information. Like an architectural blueprint, a last (traditionally made of hardwoods, like maple, but now more often of high-density plastics) provides a foundation for the shoe. Different manufacturers use different quality lasts, which impact the width, length, and fit of that brand's shoes. Some manufacturers also cut corners by substituting one last for several different styles instead of using a last that provides an exact form of the finished shoe: for example, they might use a closed-toe last to make an open-toe shoe. All of these factors add up to variable shoe sizing.

STEP 4: Try both shoes on to determine fit. You would never buy a pair of trousers after trying on one leg; the same holds true for shoes. Because of the anatomy of the body, the right and left feet are not exactly the same. You need to see how each shoe fits.

STEP 5: Match the shape of your foot to the shape of the shoe. The large, round bone where the big toe joins the foot (the ball of your foot) should be positioned above the widest part of the sole for the best medial arch support. And whether the toebox of your shoe is pointed (and no matter how pointed), round, or square, you must be able to wiggle your toes.

STEP 6: If possible, walk or stand on hard floor, not just carpet (since that is where most people spend their time walking at work, on the sidewalk, etc.). Ideally, you should walk up a staircase in the shoes to truly test the shoe (that's what we have our models do, but that's not usually possible in most shoe departments): The arch of your foot will respond to the movement, and if the shoe is fitted correctly, it will stay on without slipping off the back while you walk up and down the stairs.

STEP 7: To ensure overall comfort, make sure the shoes are properly lined. If the lining is too shiny, the foot will slide forward. If it is too stiff, the foot will feel the lining. And if the shoe is lined incorrectly (wrinkled, not glued properly, or cut too short), it will cause discomfort. Kid skins, nappa, and calf linings are your best lining choices.

Q&A

FM: What's the best style tip you ever got, and from whom?
DP: My own customers taught me that if your shoes don't fit, your personality and body will be incomplete.

FM: Define "fashion forward."
DP: Being in the right place at the right time—with the correct dress.

FM: What is your favorite fashion scene from a movie?
DP: In the remake of *The Thomas Crown Affair*, the tango scene between Pierce Brosnan and Rene Russo is the consummation of choreography and style! That is the way fashion should always be.

HOW TO BUY A CLASSIC PEARL NECKLACE

by Ella Gafter of Ella Gem NY

Ella Gafter was born in Poland during the Second World War, and out of that experience, she was determined to create beauty. As a young woman, Gafter went to Rome to learn about fine jewelry, and members of the Italian nobility were quickly drawn to the quality of her work, collecting her pieces and adopting her into their circle. Today Gafter is considered one of the world's most acclaimed pearl jewelers, and her work has been included in the pearl exhibit at the Museum of Natural History in New York City.

Pearls have been and will always be like a magnet for human beings because they are a gift of nature, spherical (the most perfect shape, according to the philosopher Plato), smooth, soft to the eye, and warm to the touch. They also produce the most wonderful sound when you play with a bunch of them in your hand. Different hues of pearl color go well with different skin colors, so every woman can wear pearls. And they match and enhance every possible style of clothing, from the most classic to the extremely fashionable.

As with any fine jewelry purchase, it makes sense to put yourself in the hands of a jeweler you trust. But a strand of pearls will be like a second skin to you, so put on the strand that most speaks to you. If you feel wonderful with it, then it's for you; if you do not, leave it, because you will not wear it! What looks and feels good is what *is* good.

STEP 1: Shape. Pearls are round by definition—therefore, the rounder the pearls in a strand, the better. However, even off-shapes—from near-round to baroque—can look great when they are charmingly matched in a strand.

STEP 2: Hue. Experience teaches that different people favor different hues. Fair-skinned people tend to look good in a pearl-white color that tends to be slightly creamy. Other types of skin often look better in "silver" hues. The optimal color, which fetches the highest prices, is an ideal pinkish with very slight silver in it.

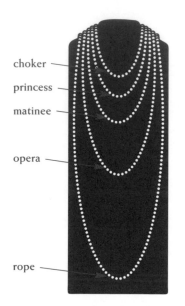

choker

princess

matinee

opera

rope

STEP 3: Length and size. The right length depends on the neck, the décolleté, the shoulders, and, of course, the clothes. The classic choice—17 to 19 inches (43–48 cm)—is referred to as princess length. It suits high as well as low necklines. Do not hesitate to ask the jeweler to shorten any strand if it looks a bit long for you. Keep the extra pearls in case you want to change the look of the strand in the future.

The right size of the pearls in your strand depends on the same factors as the length, with the addition of price. Let us just say that for a person above the age of 18 a strand of pearls smaller than 8 mm in diameter does not look good.

STEP 4: Luster. The surface or nacre of a pearl is important. Nacre is what the mollusk generates when "disturbed" by a foreign body. It manifests itself as concentric circles of white substance. Simply put, nacre is the name for the layers of skin formed around the nucleus. It must be remembered that the nacre of the pearl is the natural production of the mollusk. How can it be "perfect"? What human skin is "perfect"? Of course, the fewer blemishes, the better, like in everything else. But slight blemishes cannot take away a pearl's charm or its seductive and lively character.

What is most important is luster. We say that a pearl with no luster is like a woman without charm. Even if she is gorgeous, it won't do too much good. Luster is the level of brilliance of the pearl's skin. The crystals that form the nacre reflect and refract light (both natural and artificial). When you look at a pearl, see how much of yourself is reflected in it and to what level of detail. The more profound, rich, and mirror-like the reflection, the better the nacre and luster of the pearl.

STEP 5: Consider the classics. For a classic look, stick to Japanese pearls, South Sea pearls, and Tahitian pearls.

- **Japanese pearls** (called *akoya*, *Pinctada fucata*) range from 4 mm to 12 mm (quite rare and very expensive). These pearls typically present a nicely uniform, homogeneous look and can be worn on any occasion.

- **South Sea pearls** (*Pinctada maxima*) start at 9 mm and go up to 20 mm (very rare and super-expensive). Homogeneity is very important here, because it is harder to achieve. Therefore, when considering a strand, do your best to judge whether it is properly balanced and harmonious.

- **Tahitian pearls** (*Pinctada margaritifera*) range between 9 mm and 20 mm (rare and costly), and what you look for here is color, color, and color. The pearls must not be dark to the point of dullness; otherwise, where is the appeal? If you want a strand that will never go out of fashion, then homogeneity of color must be considered here, too.

STEP 6: Presentation. Pearls are strung with a knot separating each pearl from the next, so that if the strand breaks, you may at most have to look for one. In South Sea and Tahitian strands, the less you see the knots, the better. In Japanese strands, made with smaller pearls, you cannot not see the knots. Typically one uses silk to string Japanese strands, but silk can tear easily when you deal with bigger millimeters and higher weight. Therefore, South Sea and

Tahitian strands are typically strung on nylon, which is more resistant.

The pearl being spherical, a spherical clasp makes the most aesthetic sense. The clasp is an element of the necklace and as such must be intelligently designed to feel like an organic part of the strand. It should never look as though two disparate items were simply "stuck" together. Of course, it must be practical, which means you should not have to break your nails on it. The clasp should also have a "click" to it, so that if you close it and do not hear/feel the click, you know it has to be fixed. On the aesthetic side, it is very important that the clasp be appropriate for the necklace in size and in level of refinement. (For example, an important strand should not be accompanied by a "poor" clasp, and an everyday strand should not feature a magnificent clasp.)

Q&A

FM: Define "trendy."
EG: Several pearl necklaces worn together.

FM: Define "timeless."
EG: A strand of pearls of good size (9mm and up).

FM: Who is your favorite style icon?
EG: Coco Chanel, for creating combinations of clothes and fine jewelry that were always simple and wild at the same time.

Pearls of Wisdom

- You will know it is time to restring your pearls when the knots look slightly loose and not as "crisp" as they did when you purchased it. The loosening is the natural result of frequent wear; the weight of the pearls (particularly the larger ones) inevitably "pulls" on the knots. If you notice that the thread is dirty, restring! Again, trust your eye.

- A pearl strand goes on last and comes off first. Perfume, hairspray, and cosmetics are guaranteed to damage the luster! Put on your strand after you apply cosmetics to your face in the morning, and remove them before you cleanse your skin at night. If you use foundation/powder on your décolleté, make sure you wipe that area to remove any excess cosmetic.

- Body oils and perspiration do not really do the pearls any good (because of the toxins involved). Wash them away with a cotton cloth with a bit of warm water.

- Keep your pearls in a soft pouch. Make sure they are not "thrown together" with any other jewelry that may scratch them.

HOW TO PURCHASE VINTAGE JEWELRY

by Jill Alberts of Jill Alberts Jewelry

Jill Alberts, an estate and flea market aficionado, has an exceptional talent for selecting one-of-a-kind treasures, collecting everything from late nineteenth and early twentieth century lockets, pendants, pins, and shoe buckles to hand-painted Buddhas and Italian mosaic pieces. After taking jewelry making and design classes, Alberts turned her hobby into a business with a sale to New York's prestigious Henri Bendel. Today her designs are available nationally at specialty boutiques like Tracey Ross in Los Angeles as well as Bergdorf Goodman, Saks Fifth Avenue, and Neiman Marcus.

My introduction to vintage jewelry came from playing in my mother's and grandmother's jewelry boxes. I wore vintage clothes and costume jewelry to all my school dances, as well as through my young adult life. Today, vintage pieces are the height of modern fashion.

Costume jewelry began its modern life as "couturier jewelry," so named because it was made at the great fashion houses of designers Jean Patou and Coco Chanel in the 1920s. The simplicity of their linear designs required more flamboyant accessories, so they created exaggerated jewelry to go with their clothing. This fashion break with the repressed Victorian styles is why early costume jewelry is so opulent, like Chanel's ropes of oversized pearls studded with stones and beads. There was something a little vulgar about wearing such obviously faux jewelry, and it was a big step for women to embrace "fake jewels." But as Chanel declared, "There is no such thing as fake chic."

STEP 1: Learn the terminology. Costume jewelry, which first gained popularity in the 1920s, is jewelry that does not contain precious jewels or metals.

Collectables are those pieces manufactured after 1950. Antique costume jewelry is jewelry made before 1950; all other jewelry is considered antique if it is over 100 years old. Vintage is simply jewelry more than 50 years old.

STEP 2: Know your budget, and be prepared to invest the same amount you would spend on any piece of important jewelry. Many people who are just getting interested in vintage jewelry believe that just because a pin or a pair of earrings is old and lacks precious stones it should be inexpensive. But the rise in popularity of all levels of vintage jewelry—especially the American-made styles of the 1940s and '50s—has meant that there is no unexplored territory; there are no "steals." But vintage jewelry that appeals to you doesn't have to be a signed designer piece to be beautiful. There is still great appeal in old costume jewelry from anonymous manufacturers that you can find at smaller flea markets, secondhand stores, and rummage sales. You just have to know what to look for and what you like.

STEP 3: Strike up a conversation with the dealer. When you spot a piece you love, don't be afraid to ask questions regarding its age, quality, etc. To ensure you're dealing with a reputable dealer, ask for a business card, find out how long she has been in business, and ask whether she has a retail store you can visit. If you are shopping on eBay, look at the seller's ratings before buying.

STEP 4: Pick up the piece and inspect it carefully. Always turn the piece over and look underneath. Is it stamped by the manufacturer or signed by the artist? Often, when no trademark or designer name can be found, many collectors will discard the piece. However, buying vintage is not an exact science: Some actual designer pieces were not stamped and some very beautiful pieces are not designer. I believe you should buy a piece based on its design and beauty, even if the collector doesn't value it highly.

STEP 5: On a bracelet or necklace, take a look at the catch. Does it match the piece, or can you see that it has been replaced? If the catch is original and matches, it can tell you its approximate age: From 1840 to 1900, the "C" catch was used. It is a curved catch (shaped like the letter "C") or a hook, where the pin is tucked inside the curve to close it. In 1910, the invention of a closure to hold the pin in place was introduced as a "safety catch." The modern safety catch, still in use today, is a more refined version in which the closure holds the "C" in place without protruding; it dates back to the early 1930s. Jewelry with its original catch will have more value than a piece with a replacement catch.

STEP 6: Check out the weight to date the piece. As a general rule, older pieces are heavier and more primitive in details and base metals (using nonprecious materials, such as copper instead of gold). Gauging the weight and knowing the base metal will help you date the piece to a particular decade. (See sidebar on opposite page). Checking out museum exhibits and old magazine advertisements will also help show what women were wearing in certain time periods and can assist you in identifying the proper period for the piece you're interested in.

STEP 7: Check to see if all the stones are original. Are they the same color, or do the colors vary? Are there new soldering or glue marks that give away a replaced or repaired stone? Are they in place? Have they been soldered (indicating higher quality craftsmanship) or only glued? Give them a wiggle. If stones are loose, it is easy to tighten them by using small-nosed pliers. You can use this to your advantage as a bartering point if you can repair the loose stone yourself or if the idea of losing the stone doesn't bother you.

STEP 8: Don't be afraid to bargain! Ask, "What's the best price you can give me?" and "What if I buy more than one?" Many dealers will negotiate, but some dealers set firm prices and will not waver. If you truly want the piece, be prepared to pay the asking price.

Identifying Period Pieces by Design

Use the following "cheat sheet" to identify the vintage period and piece.

- **Art Nouveau** (1895–1910) designs were centered on poetic interpretations of nature—the lines were curved, with natural motifs, intertwining floral patterns, butterflies. Stones of the earth, such as opals, pearls, and moonstones were used.

- **Edwardian** (1901–1915) pieces are light, lacy, feminine designs, typified by the white-on-white look of pearls, diamonds, and platinum.

- **Art Deco** (1915–1930) designs incorporate geometric lines, bold colors, and the use of platinum, white gold, silver, emeralds, ruby, sapphire, onyx, diamonds, and rock crystal.

- **Retro** (1935–1950) jewelry is oversized and feminine, employing designs that copy the jewelry of previous periods (like Art Deco or Art Nouveau). Rubies and other stones are frequently used.

edwardian

retro

art nouveau

art deco

⚠ **"How do I clean my vintage rhinestone jewelry without damaging it?"** The greatest threat to costume jewelry is moisture. If your piece has rhinestones, never immerse it in liquid; it will lose its foil backing and be permanently damaged. Instead, fill a container with a good glass cleaner and dip a small, clean, soft-bristle toothbrush into the liquid. Brush the piece gently. Do not let the liquid seep into the setting, as it can eat away the backing and ruin the brilliance of the rhinestones. Dry with a soft cloth.

EXTRA HELP

Jewelry Terms:

Repousse (embossing) is a decorative technique for raising a pattern on metal by beating, punching, or hammering from the reverse side.

Parure is a complete set of jewelry, usually consisting of a necklace, earrings, brooch, and bracelet.

A demi-parure (a set) is two matching pieces of the same design.

Q&A

FM: Define "timeless."
JA: My grandmother's 14-karat gold charm bracelet.

FM: Who's your favorite style icon?
JA: No one does vintage like Kate Moss. She always looks amazing and unique.

FM: What's your favorite fashion scene from a movie?
JA: Pistol-toting Faye Dunaway in *Bonnie and Clyde*—her beret, perfectly bobbed hair, tweed pencil skirt. She is timelessly beautiful, crazy in love, and tough as hell!

How to Start
a Charm Bracelet

by Annoushka Ducas of Links of London

Annoushka Ducas is the cofounder and creative director of Links of London, an international retailer of luxury jewelry and accessories. After graduating from the Sorbonne in Paris, Ducas began designing jewelry in her spare time in Hong Kong. The success of her early work (sold in the prestigious lifestyle store Harvey Nichols) inspired Ducas to open her first freestanding store in Broadgate, London's financial district. Links of London has stores around the world.

A charm bracelet is more than a piece of jewelry—it can be a special part of your life. You can acquire charms to mark your memories, inscribe your dreams, and reveal the spirit within. Adding charms to your bracelet can be part of the way in which you celebrate your achievements and recall the most precious people, places, and pets you have known. A charm bracelet has the power to tell the story of your life and makes an incredibly sentimental family heirloom.

STEP 1: Decide between gold and silver. Naturally, gold bracelets require gold charms, and silver bracelets require silver charms. The appeal of a silver charm bracelet is that it develops an increased patina, making it all the more desirable and adding to the personality of the piece. Gold is more expensive than silver, but it does not tarnish and can look spectacular for day-into-night pieces.

STEP 2: Choose the bracelet. The basic bracelet on which you hang your charms should be simple and well made with a reliable clasp. While Links carries the signature toggle fastening, two other clasp styles are the slide clasp and the spring ring. The latter two clasps should also have a chain guard that attaches to both ends of the bracelet in case the catch should open accidentally.

In order to select the proper bracelet, consider how many charms you would like to have as well as the average size of the charms you fancy. The size and number of links in the bracelet should correspond. For example, a bracelet of triple interlocking links can support bigger and bolder charms and is also a good choice if you like the look of many charms. A bracelet of two interlocking links is better for fewer, lighter charms or a child's collection.

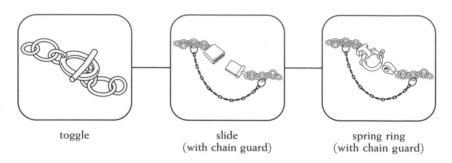

toggle

slide
(with chain guard)

spring ring
(with chain guard)

STEP 3: Select your approach—gradual or themed. If you plan on building your bracelet slowly over time to commemorate milestones in your life, start off with a personalized and engraved disc or heart, or a charm that marks a celebration, like those that signify the birth of a child, perhaps a baby lamb or a diamond bootie.

You can also build a theme bracelet quickly, inspired by the passions in your life, like assembling charms in the shape of a mobile phone, lipsticks, Jackie O. sunglasses, lucky panties, a killer heel shoe, a "big rock" ring, and a cocktail glass.

STEP 4: Arrange and attach the charms to the bracelet. To arrange the charms, lay your bracelet out on a flat surface and position your charms, moving them about until you get a good chronological arrangement (from the first to most recent purchase to trace events in your life, like charms to commemorate your engagement, marriage, anniversary) or an eye-pleasing aesthetic.

Charms are attached to your bracelet with jump rings (loops that secure the charm to the bracelet). Although many can be opened and closed by hand with a pair of pliers (and some are split rings, like a smaller version of key rings), the safest way to attach your charms is to have them soldered by a jeweler (most will do so for a nominal fee).

STEP 5: Care for the bracelet. Charm bracelets made of metal only (like silver or 18-karat gold) can be dipped into a jewelry cleaning solution. However, before proceeding, check that the charms do not contain any hollow areas that might trap fluid—solvent solution trapped inside a charm will discolor the metal. The charm bracelet must only be placed in the solution for approximately 30 seconds, then thoroughly rinsed off in a weak lukewarm clothing detergent solution and passed under warm tap water. Dry with a soft cloth. Once completely dried, the bracelet can be buffed lightly with a polish-impregnated polishing cloth. If the bracelet's discoloration is only minimal, a clean polishing cloth may be enough to clean the piece.

Charms with stones may also be cleaned with a lukewarm clothing detergent solution. However, soft stones (like pearl, Mother of Pearl, malachite, lapis, turquoise) are much more porous than hard stones (diamonds, rubies, sapphires) and should be cleaned with a very soft bristle brush.

Q&A

FM: Define "timeless."
AD: A black cashmere sweater—a staple item in anyone's wardrobe.

FM: What's the best style tip you ever got, and from whom?
AD: My own advice is that accessories are the key to individuality.

FM: What's your favorite fashion scene from a movie?
AD: Grace Kelly in *Rear Window*—the whole movie is Grace Kelly and her wardrobe. It's hard to pick a favorite scene, but I would have to opt for the first vision of Grace reflected in the window. The charm bracelet she wore in the film set off a huge fashion moment in the 1950s.

How to Choose an Overcoat

by Rick Weinstein of Searle

Rick Weinstein is the director of sales and marketing for Searle, a coat design firm and retailer with eight shops in New York City. Weinstein has traveled the country representing Searle, helping thousands of customers purchase fashionable coats in Bergdorf Goodman, Saks Fifth Avenue, Neiman Marcus, Bloomingdale's, Nordstrom, and many other fine stores.

No wardrobe can be complete without the classic winter overcoat. As a staple, your overcoat is an investment piece. It's the first thing people see, and because of that, no matter how well dressed you are underneath it, your coat makes your biggest fashion statement. If you make the right selection—a classic cut in what is a neutral color for the rest of your wardrobe—you will wear a coat for years, adding accessories like hats and scarves and brooches for up-to-the minute fashion variety.

Before you go out shopping for a coat, put on clothes that are typical of what you'll wear underneath it, like a sweater or a blazer. Here are the factors you should keep in mind during your search.

STEP 1: Consider your body proportions. Every woman wants a coat that makes her look longer and leaner. Focus on the proportions, trying on different styles until you find the one that flatters your figure. Experimenting is crucial because there is a coat out there with the proper proportions for any height. Here are some general guidelines:

- **Short:** A woman who is only 5 feet (1.5 m) tall will not look good in a 7/8-length coat because it cuts her off in the wrong place. But by purchasing a coat that stops at the knee, her lower leg will be accentuated, which, to the eye, makes her look taller.
- **Tall:** A tall woman needs to find a coat with proportions that befit her

vertical challenge. If she's purchasing a long coat, it must be at least 53 inches (1.3 m) long to look right. A maxi coat is too short; it looks like she's wearing someone else's coat. A 7/8-length coat on most people will be a 3/4-length on her, just reaching her knee. So she has to shop accordingly, to find the proportion that gives her a look that is appropriate for her height.

- **Full Figure:** A woman who cannot wear a fitted coat can create the illusion of looking long and lean in a coat that skims her body, rather than the A-line silhouette she may be tempted to purchase. The A-line is defensive dressing—anyone can throw on a huge coat, but what are you achieving? It's akin to wearing a tent. The "close-to-the-body" coat is going on the offense, in the sense that the woman is making an effort to show herself in the best light.

STEP 2: Consider the color. Everyone has colors that look best on them. A woman who has olive skin can wear an olive green coat very well, whereas that same shade can appear yellowish on a person with pale skin. If you don't know what colors work well for you, find a consultant in your favorite store who you can trust to lead you to the color promised land.

STEP 3: Consider the durability of the fabric Fabrics all have their virtues and shortcomings. It all comes down to whether the coat is going to be your everyday coat or one among many. If this coat is for everyday wear, you need a fabric that is durable. Alpaca, baby llama, and cashmere are luxurious fabrics that are blended with wool to give years of wearability. Nylon and polyester are no longer bad words—blends of these materials also add to the durability of fabrics without detracting from their hand (feel) and appearance.

STEP 4: Consider the sleeve. The way the sleeve is set will determine how much mobility you have in the coat. A deep dolman (a full sleeve that is very wide at the armhole and narrow at the wrist) or raglan sleeve (extends in one piece to the neckline of the coat) provide far more mobility than a very high set version (set on top or at the edge of the shoulder, to give your coat a narrow look). But a woman who likes the look of a fitted coat will rarely consider either. Some coats may have a half dolman sleeve, which appears set in the front yet is roomy in the rear.

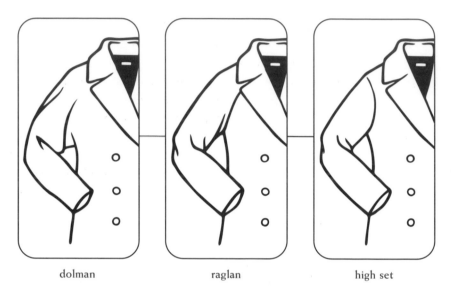

| dolman | raglan | high set |

STEP 5: Consider the quality. Quality construction is fairly obvious to determine.

- Do the seams meet?
- Are the buttons fastened well and are the buttonholes clean and neat?
- Are there threads hanging out?
- Is the hem straight?
- Is the lining hanging below the bottom?

After the obvious, quality becomes subjective. If you're buying the coat to last, details matter.

- Do the buttons look appropriate on the coat? Are they sturdy, or will they cut the thread and fall off or break?
- Is the shoulder pad too big? Does it extend over the edge of your shoulder, preventing the coat from fitting properly? Does the coat need to be taken in across the midsection? And is it worth spending extra money to make it fit as it should, not only keeping you warm but showing you to your best advantage?

STEP 6: Consider the length. There are three considerations when it comes to the length of a coat, all more important than the latest fashion. What is your height (see step 1)? What is your lifestyle? Do you get cold?
- If you're a suburban mom who spends most of her time getting in and out of cars, car coat length is the length for you.
- If you're an urbanite who walks all the time, you need at least a $3/4$ or $7/8$ length, but not full length, because you'll step on it when getting on the bus or train.
- If you're a salesperson who spends all your time going from customer to customer, a full length coat will shield you from the elements.

Q&A

FM: Define "timeless."
RW: Black cashmere.

FM: What's the worst fashion faux pas?
RW: Leaving the content label on the sleeves for the duration to tell the world it's cashmere.

FM: What's your favorite fashion scene from a movie?
RW: Any scene from *Sleepless in Seattle*, the raincoat's finest hour.

Finding the Perfect Fit

We notice that customers tend to do more physical activity while trying on a coat than they typically do in their everyday lives—things like raising their hands straight in the air, swinging their arms wildly, and touching their toes are but a few of the preparations taken when selecting a coat. It reminds me of the doctor whose patient says, "It hurts when I do this." His quick retort is, "Then don't do it."

The truth actually falls somewhere in the middle. A style-devotee who wears a very fitted coat is willing to live by the axiom, "fashion is pain." But the typical customer just wants to be comfortable when driving or slinging her bag over her shoulder. Go with what works for you.

HOW TO BUNDLE UP WITHOUT LOOKING LIKE A WALRUS

by Joni Wilkins of Ramosport USA

Former interior designer Joni Wilkins closed the doors of her successful firm and put her experience, love of fashion, and passion for style to work on a new venture by launching the Ramosport brand in the USA. A company that can trace its Russian roots back to making impermeable jackets for the troops of the tsar's army, Ramosport's stylish coats for inclement weather are available at Bergdorf Goodman, Saks Fifth Avenue, Nordstrom, and many more fine clothing stores. Wilkins is currently a partner and the Vice President of Ramosport USA.

It doesn't matter how long the winter cold snap lasts in your particular part of the country—even one day is too long if you're not properly dressed. For those women who experience a long winter season, dressing to protect themselves from the elements and still holding to some semblance of fashion (especially urbanites who spend time waiting on train platforms and walking along windy city blocks) is winter's greatest challenge. But how can you layer clothing to stay warm when you already feel as though you're carrying around a little extra padding?

STEP 1: Your bottom layer is your bottom layer, so why not make it beautiful? We all know that underpinnings set your mental state, and there's no reason to sacrifice femininity during colder weather.

STEP 2: Start with the top of your body. Begin with a single-layer silk crewneck shirt with long sleeves and snug wrists or cuffs—once you get a wind tunnel up your sleeves, your entire torso is cold.

Build upon that layer with a sweater (perhaps a turtleneck) or blouse, as long as that garment is tapered and formfitting. Relax, no one is asking you to go "tight"—just avoid anything square, boxy, or too heavily knit in favor of a garment with shape. Anyone who has ever owned a good-quality Merino wool or cashmere sweater can attest that the size of your sweater doesn't relate to its ability to keep you warm. And once you add a bulky sweater, where can you go after that?

STEP 3: Move on to the bottom. If you are wearing slacks, the key to warmth without bulk is lightweight hose under the pants, thin socks over the hose, and boots. A great pair of lined wool slacks will keep you warm, but avoid pleated pants in favor of those with a leaner, cleaner cut.

If you are wearing a skirt, you have the freedom to choose a heavier pair of tights. Of course, the longer the skirt, the more warmth it will provide. Avoid an A-line skirt that "balloons" in favor of a pencil skirt (preferably lined to avoid ugly static cling) that will stay closer to the body and elongate your line. Again, fabrics are very important for warmth, and wool or wool blends will do the trick.

Finish off either look with boots, boots, and boots! Good leather boots will keep your feet and calves warm, and keeping your selection tonal (in the same color family as your skirts or slacks) will help to create a long clean vision. Good quality socks go a long way as well. Cashmere are the best—they are warm and dreamy to wear. Just be careful when putting them on—pull them over your feet gently, as the heels can easily wear out.

STEP 4: Finish with outerwear. When it comes to your top or coat layer, shape isn't just important, it's critical. Keep your coat close to the body, and if you find the right length, that layer will decrease rather than increase your bulky look. Although the proper length depends on your height and body proportions (are you short-waisted or long-waisted? what is the ratio of your limb length to your torso?), here are general rules that apply to everyone:

- **For sportier dressing** (car coat length or above), a jacket/coat that is too short increases the width of your "middle" (and creates the dreaded "bagel" effect), while one that lands directly on your hips accents your hips. However, when you overcompensate and go too long, you lose the sporty effect and begin to tip over into career dressing. The most flattering sporty look that is also functional is a coat approximately 30 to 33 inches (76–84 cm) from the center of the back of your neck, depending upon your height. The coat should land mid-thigh, an easy length for getting in and out of a car, which is why this length is affectionately known as a "soccer mom" coat.
- **For a career look**, you want a full-length coat (landing just above or just below the knee) with straight lines: nothing A-line; nothing short and swingy. A coat with invisible (or inside) darts can help provide shape.

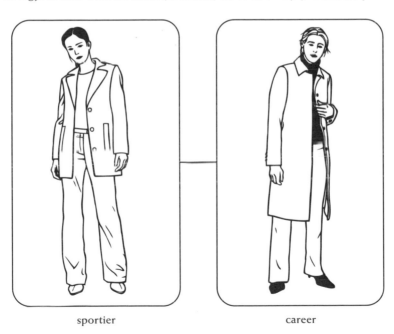

sportier   career

With outerwear, keep things tonal to your wardrobe (for example, a dark green coat if you wear a lot of earth colors) to enhance the illusion of vertical lines. Once you start visually drawing a horizontal line across your body by breaking colors (for example a royal blue parka over brown pants), you only look wider.

Q&A

FM: What's the best style tip you ever got, and from whom?
JW: My mom taught me to buy beautiful wardrobe pieces instead of going for abundance.

FM: Who is film's most fashionable leading man?
JW: Will Smith, because he can wear any style.

FM: Who is your favorite style icon?
JW: Anna Wintour: She's an encyclopedia of fashion, culture, and art.

How to Tie a Scarf Like a French Woman

by Mireille Guiliano of Clicquot Inc.

Mireille Guiliano, cofounder, president, CEO, and U.S. spokesperson for Champagne Veuve Clicquot of Reims, France, was raised on the world's most famous wine and is regarded as a leading expert on champagne. A native of France and student of the Sorbonne, she has contributed articles on wine, food, and travel to Town & Country *and is the author of* French Women Don't Get Fat, *a mix of memoir, advice, recipes, lifestyle tips, and cross-cultural commentary.*

French women collect scarves the way American women collect shoes or handbags. It's the "must-have" accessory, as it can transform any outfit into a fresh one and signal a mood. If one can only have one, it would have to be the square silk scarf (30 to 36 inches [76–91 cm] square, depending on the brand). When scarves get big enough, we call them shawls (cashmere being the material of choice) and play with them. I always like to have one with me when I wear an evening dress. The French woman's secret is to tie it with "nonchalance"—to keep it loose and give the impression that it's just there and part of you

FOR A WINTER COAT OR WITH A BLAZER

Choose a large scarf, about 40 inches (1 m) square.

STEP 1: Create an oblong shape by folding the opposite sides of the scarf inward, repeating until the scarf is a manageable width.

STEP 2: Place the middle of the scarf at the back of the neck, crossing the ends over in the front.

STEP 3: Allow the lapels of your coat or jacket to hold the scarf in place, adjusting the fabric to fill in the neckline.

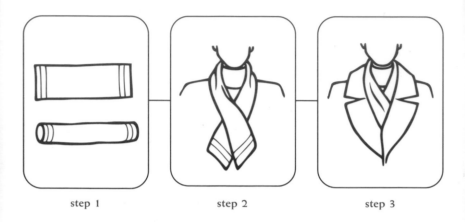

step 1   step 2   step 3

FOR A CLASSIC DRESS

Choose a large scarf, about 40 inches (1 m) square.

STEP 1: Fold two opposite ends of the scarf into the center, one after the other. Continue folding in these sides until the scarf is a manageable width.

STEP 2: Place the middle of the scarf at the back of your neck, with both ends hanging down in front.

STEP 3: Loosely loop one end of the scarf over the other and gently tighten until the fold is lying at the base of your throat.

STEP 4: Tie a loose knot, tightening as needed. Spread the fabric to fit your the neckline, letting ends hang down, or tuck the ends into the band of the scarf to create a knotted circlet. Adjust to fit your neckline.

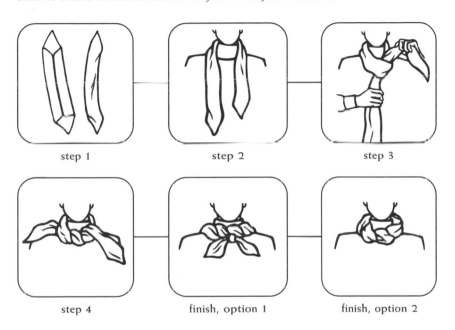

step 1   step 2   step 3

step 4   finish, option 1   finish, option 2

FOR LONG SCARVES OR CASHMERE SHAWLS

Choose a rectangular scarf measuring about two by five feet (.6 x 1.5 m). The fabric should not be too bulky; silk or lightweight wool or cashmere works best.

STEP 1: Softly gather the scarf horizontally with both hands and fold it in half lengthwise. You now have a loop on one side and two loose ends on the other.

STEP 2: Hold the scarf around the back of your neck, extending the loop on one side and the two loose ends on the other.

STEP 3: Slip the two loose ends through the loop to form a makeshift knot, adjusting until the knot is snug.

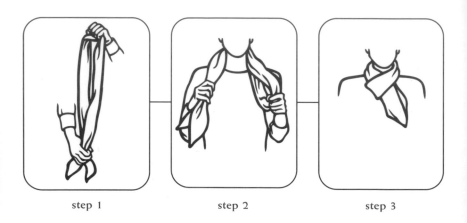

step 1   step 2   step 3

Q&A

FM: What's the best style tip you ever got, and from whom?
MG: One can go far with a great haircut, a bottle of vintage champagne, and a divine perfume, from my mother; and from my godmother, that the little black dress is a must in your wardrobe.

FM: Define "fashion forward."
MG: Mixing textures, patterns, styles, breaking the rules, and understated elegance.

FM: Define "timeless."
MG: Love, black, white, a pearl necklace, Chanel No. 5.

How to Become a Hat Person

by Ellen Christine Colon-Lugo of Ellen Christine Millinery

Philadelphia-born Ellen Christine Colon-Lugo apprenticed to a tailor before turning her talents to millinery. While working in Boston, she bought a socialites' collection of 350 hats, perfecting her craft by taking the hats apart and reconstructing them. An eminent authority on costume design, Colon-Lugo holds a master's and doctorate in the subject from New York University. Her hats can be seen in the fashion spreads of magazines like Vogue *and* Vanity Fair, *as well as in her eclectic New York retail store.*

Even if you've never, ever thought of wearing one, it's a fact: Every face has a hat. Period. Your job is to find the one that fits yours, but you're not likely to make that happen in a millinery department of a large department store. They are typically small, with a limited selection and a cookie-cutter approach: Every hat looks about the same. And bear in mind that a hat is not a sock—I am not talking about a knitted version that is pulled down over your eyes. A hat should have shape and form and color; it should be something you can play with.

It also helps to get your expectations on straight. A hat won't hide your nose or disguise any flaws you might think you have. A hat is supposed to frame your face, and when you find one that does, it will make your eyes light up. That's the hat for you.

STEP 1: Go shopping alone. Finding the right hat for your face—especially for first-timers—is a time-intensive process, and you don't want to have to shift your focus away from yourself to deal with anyone else's needs or schedules or opinions. Selfish? Maybe. But efficient. And do it now. Don't wait for a special occasion. Nothing is harder to find than the right hat when you need the right hat.

STEP 2: Wear lipstick. You are going to spend most of the time peering in the mirror and need a positive frame of reference for your face. Colored lips (whatever your shade might be) give you a place to focus. Your hair should be clean and arranged in your normal style.

STEP 3: Investigate your hat style. Go someplace (or if you can find them, several places) where they have lots of different hat styles. Avoid department stores (because they are not geared to individual style) in favor of someplace intimate—a bona fide milliner or a specialty hat shop—where they have mirrors and good lighting. Try on everything.

Most first-time hat wearers—I call them "hat virgins"—automatically reach for something black because they want to "match" a black coat or suit, and it's safe. The truth is that not everyone should surround herself in a mass of black, and besides, trying on a hat that isn't black will help you to see the actual shape of it.

STEP 4: Start simple. The first hat that most women attempt is the classic beret (think Faye Dunaway as Bonnie in *Bonnie and Clyde*) because it is easy to wear and after that, its cousin, the cloche. This is a bell-shaped hat made of fabric or felt reminiscent of twenties flapper style (think Renée Zellweger as Roxy Hart in *Chicago*). These are both styles that hug the head and don't involve a dramatic shape.

STEP 5: Extend your search to brimmed hats. The more evolved hat style will have a brim and a flat or round crown. Try on both crown styles to determine which is right for you. This is a matter of proportion, focusing on the width and length of your face and the shape of your head. There are as many variations of this combination as there are people, so the only general guidelines are to try on both crown styles and look in the mirror from all angles. The crown should flatter your profile as well.

Finding the type of crown that works for the size and shape of your head narrows your search down to what size brim is appropriate for your face, and here you must study the proportions between the size of the brim and your facial structure, focusing on three places—the cheekbones, nose, and chin. Again, variables abound. But generally speaking it's a matter of geometry: Long narrow faces won't work with a tall, thin hat; a round facial structure won't do as well with a bowler. This is where access to many shapes and the time to try them on pays off. It helps to focus on the arch of your eyebrow and follow that line up to the hat. If that line looks pleasing to the eye, so will the brim of the hat in proportion to your facial structure.

However, the brim should NOT extend beyond the shoulder (don't laugh: Victorian ladies went overboard with this one!), and, if you run into trouble, do as my grandmother always said: Give it a dip! The diagonal always helps different proportion faces, admits light to the eye area, and, above all, won't get in the way of your food!

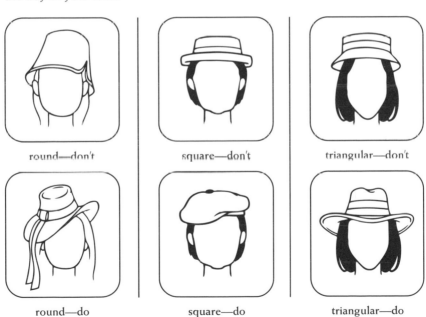

round—don't

square—don't

triangular—don't

round—do

square—do

triangular—do

⚠ **"Help—I have hat hair!"** Okay, hat hair: Must I hear that phrase every day of my life? I have a little trick for those of you with long hair: Take a small bit of hair near the crown, twirl it around and pin it into a chignon (on the crown) before you put on your hat. Not only will you have a place to put your hatpin (the chignon will provide a good anchor), but when you take the hat off and unpin the chignon, the top layer of your hair will be wavy and full, and voilà: no hat hair. On the other hand, since so many of us do the straightening thing (with an iron) to flatten our hair, a hat can help maintain the straight line.

Those of you with short hair should ruffle your hair after removing the hat and then leave it alone; too much fussing only makes it worse.

Q&A

FM: Define "fashion forward."
ECCL: Ankle socks with high heels.

FM: Who is film's most fashionable leading lady?
ECCL: Norma Shearer, probably best known for her roles as Mary Haines in George Cukor's catfight classic *The Women*. She was not your everyday movie star.

FM: Who is film's most fashionable leading man?
ECCL: Danny Kaye, because he matched his socks to his suede shoes and his trouser so when he twirled around in his dance numbers you saw one continuous line.

How to Get a Handle on Your Handbag Wardrobe

by Rafe Totengco of Rafe New York

Using his Pan-International perspective, Philippine-native Rafe Totengco, founder and designer of Rafe New York, takes simple shapes beyond basic with his use of restrained embellishments like embroidery, beading, and leather accents. His bag and accessory lines for both women and men are hailed by industry insiders as "redefined classics," and Totengco was recently given the ACE Award for Best Accessories Designer, a tribute to his flawless style and unbridled creativity.

In a way, the modern woman's handbag is like her armor. It's one of the first things you notice (or not, depending on her choice of bag), and every bag says something about the lifestyle, sense of aesthetics, and personality of the woman wearing it. Black says safe, color says individualistic, crocodile says luxury, nylon says practical, animal print says "notice me," a little print says sweet, handheld says prissy, and over-the-shoulder says no fuss.

Naturally, you will encounter variables in quality along the way, but if you are serious about building a collection of handbags in classic shapes, investing in one "good" bag per category makes the most sense. The bag should be well made and of high-quality materials—examine the stitching and the hardware, and feel the materials used inside and out, including lining and interior pockets. Stitching should be even and straight, the hardware should be evenly finished without any scratches, and the closures must be conveniently positioned and durable in construction. Quality leather usually feels supple to the touch and malleable in your hand. Depending on the finish, certain leathers feel waxy or silky.

There will always be an of-the-season handbag that you crave—be it a signature shape, an animal print, real fur, bead encrusted, or simply because Kate Moss is wearing it—but the major bags in your wardrobe should fall into five style categories.

THE HOBO BAG

COMMON FEATURES: Named for the tied-up cloth sack that a hobo slings over a shoulder to carry belongings, this is a slouchy and roomy bag, intended for the most casual dressing.

Usually shaped a bit like a pear, the hobo bag can be made of soft nappa leather (calfskin) or suede, but is also cute in an unexpected fabrication like velvet or crochet. The bag is often softly gathered at the bottom seam (so it can expand) with a zippered closure and a sturdy interior lining that is slightly suspended above the actual shape of the bag (not only as protection from stains but so the weight of your belongings does not stretch the soft leather or suede). There is typically a short shoulder strap (often made from the same fabric as the bag) that may or may not tie on top of the shoulder (calling to mind the hobo's pouch), but in any case, should be adjustable.

WHAT TO LOOK FOR: Look for a zippered interior pocket to hold what you use most, so things like keys and phones don't get lost in the bottom of the bag. Most designer bags have pleated pockets for a mobile phone, PDAs, and other items.

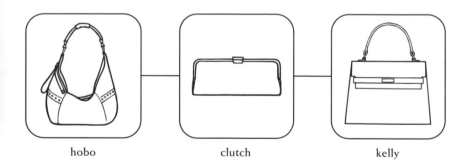

hobo   clutch   kelly

THE CLUTCH

COMMON FEATURES: A handheld clutch is an elegant, ladylike look. This sort of bag is appropriate for any night out, whether you're going to a black tie event or a casual dinner date.

Clutches typically come with a metal frame and a drop-in chain (to act as a handle, always a nice option), but sometimes a clutch is styled like an envelope, with a fold-over flap and a magnetic snap or a decorative jewel closure (rarely with detachable straps). Sizes vary, but the majority of clutches are small and easy to hold in the palm of your hand, hence the name clutch. They usually have enough room for lipstick, some money, keys, and a mobile phone.

WHAT TO LOOK FOR: Safer choices come in black satin, but I prefer beaded, embroidered, a fabulous silk brocade in a multicolor pattern, or an exotic skin like python or crocodile. Metallics are a basic—a gold leather clutch is a great start to your collection because it goes with everything.

TOP HANDLE OR KELLY BAG

COMMON FEATURES: Perhaps more than any other style of handbag, the top-handled Kelly represents an investment piece. As a fashion talisman, this handbag is endlessly versatile and eternally elegant.

French luxury leather house Hermès named a top-handled bag after Hollywood film star Grace Kelly, who became Her Serene Highness Princess of Monaco. The Kelly became a style icon in 1956, when a photograph of Princess Grace carrying one appeared on the cover of *Life* magazine (rumor is that she used it to hide the bulge that would later reveal to the world she was pregnant). Ever since then, any small, top-handled bag has been called a Kelly, even if it isn't made by Hermès.

WHAT TO LOOK FOR: When selecting a top handle bag, look for quality, quality, quality, as it will never go out of style. Start with a strap that is a perfect width for your hand grip (as this is not a shoulder bag), sturdy metal frame, a solidly made and secure closure, wall pockets that lay flat (against the interior sides of the purse), smoothly fitting lining, and even stitching.

THE SHOULDER BAG

COMMON FEATURES: The shoulder bag, made popular in the forties during the war when women joined the workforce and realized their little clutch bags were not designed to hold all their possessions, is an extremely broad category. However, it essentially can be recognized by a flap-over to close the bag (covering 3/4 of the front), a single sling shoulder strap (adjustable and with a buckle), and one or two external pockets for easy access. This bag (sometimes called a saddle bag) can be worn across the body or hanging from one shoulder.

WHAT TO LOOK FOR: It pays to remember that this is not a tote bag. Your shoulder bag should still fall into the handbag—not suitcase—category.

TOTE

COMMON FEATURES: A tote is a must for someone who carries a lot on a daily basis. You'll want two: one for casual wear, and one for work. Totes are typically handheld and big enough to carry a load of papers, folders, magazines, and even an extra pair of shoes. Since this bag takes an extra beating, a tote usually comes in treated canvas or nylon and sometimes in heavy pebbled leather. A work tote would be a little more constructed, sized to accommodate a legal folder and with enough inside pockets to store your PDA, a slim laptop, and even extra pockets for pens and a metro card. (Some versions come with an inside zipper compartment in the center that divides the bag in sections.)

WHAT TO LOOK FOR: The canvas boat tote (whether open or with a zipper closure) is the perfect example of a casual tote. Look for heavyweight canvas that has been treated for water repellency and stitched with a heavy-duty nylon thread for extra durability.

For a work tote, look for a textured leather (so that the scratches that will happen with daily wear and tear don't show up immediately) in a basic black or brown color (since you want this bag to go with everything you own). The linings should feel strong when you tug on them, and if possible, the fabric should have a non-fray finish (as most quality makers use). Luxury companies may also use pig suede or leather for inside lining. Make sure the tote has bottom studs or "feet" to minimize extra scratching that comes with daily use. The shoulder straps should be long enough and set far enough apart that you are comfortable when wearing a jacket or coat. (If the bag causes your garments to bunch up on the shoulders, then it's not the right tote for you). Some women prefer handheld totes as an alternative because shoulder totes can destroy the line of your jacket.

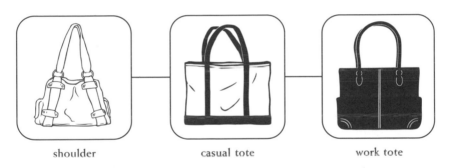

shoulder   casual tote   work tote

FM: Define "trendy."

RT: Hippie fringe bags. These always get resurrected every few years but never seem to have any staying power unless your role model is Janis Joplin.

FM: Define "timeless."

RT: The LL Bean canvas boat tote. Trends come and go, and this remains. It's such a classic design that many designers have done their version of it.

FM: What's the best style tip you ever got, and from whom?

RT: My father gave me a plaque to hang on my wall that said, "Fine clothes may disguise, but silly words will disclose a fool." I've always remembered that and live by it: No matter how fabulously dressed you are, education is the best accessory.

EXTRA HELP

Is This the Bag for You?

Before making your final decision, "try on" the handbag, just as you would a pair of shoes or a jacket. Transfer your wallet, keys, and cosmetic bag into it. Grasp the handles (or position the strap over your shoulder) and look at yourself in a full-length mirror. As an outward sign of your personal style, the bag should meld with your wardrobe and be in proportion to your size. And just like any other key fashion garment, you should consider your classic handbags an investment. After all, a bargain bag that sits on your shelf because it's just "not you" isn't much of a bargain after all.

How to Carry a Computer Bag and Still Look Good

by Molly Nelson and Katherine Walker of MARKA

MARKA founders Molly Nelson, former director of strategy for Old Navy, and Katherine Walker, former business development manager for Lilly Pulitzer, met at Stanford Business School. While logging countless hours of travel with masculine, unwieldy, and impractical laptop bags in their jobs, they spotted the need for a fresh, fashionable, and functional alternative. They developed MARKA to meet the needs of today's professional woman with luxurious and comfortable handbags—all named after their old boyfriends.

Today's woman is always on the go, and since you don't have time to change bags in the course of a given day, it's key to find a bag that is suited to multiple environments. Your briefcase/computer bag is an extension of your appearance and should align with the rest of your professional wardrobe in terms of color and fabrication.

Computer bags and briefcases incorporating classic colors, fundamental wardrobe hues, and luxurious materials are appropriate in the most conservative office as well as in an elegant after-work setting. Select colors or patterns that complement the rest of your wardrobe as well as trimmings that reflect your own style preferences. Do you like lots of bells and whistles, like decorative zippers and rivets, or is your look more sleek and minimalist? The bag you select must blend the elements of luxury, functionality, style, and comfort.

STEP 1: Look for a bag that weighs no more than 4 pounds (1.8 kg). The majority of computer bags weigh 6 to 7 pounds (2.7–3.1 kg) empty. Given that the average laptop weighs 6 pounds (2.7 kg), this combined weight can quickly become excessive once the rest of your everyday items are placed in the bag.

STEP 2: Choose materials that are lightweight and easy to care for. Materials like canvas and nylon are much lighter than most bags made of leather. Look for materials treated with stain- and water-repellant finishes that will keep bags looking fresh and clean, particularly when traveling. Avoid fabrications, trims, and hard edges that can snag clothing easily; Velcro can quickly ruin a beautiful suit or a delicate blouse.

STEP 3: Choose a bag that provides ample protection for your laptop. Look for heavy-duty foam padding; linings should be soft to avoid scratching your computer, yet durable enough to withstand taking the laptop in and out of the case thousands of times. Removable insert cases will make it much easier to access your laptop prior to entering the security lines at airports.

STEP 4: Make sure the bag's design incorporates plenty of easy-access pockets for your everyday essentials, as well as a sufficient number of compartments for stowing other items you take to and from work or on errands each day. We recommend that you take all of the items out of your current bag, identify the "everyday essentials," and let the type of pockets and compartments needed to accommodate them drive your purchase decision (see "Bag Compartment Checklist," p. 144). For example, many women also use their computer case as a briefcase and need space for legal files, magazines, and cosmetics.

STEP 5: Look for a bag with a removable, adjustable shoulder strap that you can tailor to your height and body shape. A computer shoulder strap should be padded (so it doesn't move around too easily) and lay flat (tubular straps are popular and stylish but often dig into the shoulder under excessive weight and become very uncomfortable). It should adjust to a length that slides easily over a winter coat without being long enough to flap around at your hip, which creates more strain on the back by placing weight below your center of gravity. (There is nothing quite like running through an airport at full speed with your bag banging on your hip with each step you take.) The materials used should be sturdy enough to withstand the weight of your computer, soft and smooth enough to avoid snagging a beautiful jacket or top, and durable enough to look "worn in" rather than "old" after years of use.

STEP 6: Make sure your bag also has double loop handles long enough to slide over your shoulder that are securely attached to the bag with strong hardware. A bag handle that is approximately 9^1/$_2$ to 10 inches (24–25 cm) long will easily slide over your shoulder and help keep the bag tucked under the arm at your side. This is much more comfortable and makes it easier to control the bag's movement. Double loop handles should be attached with rings or buckles and secured by sturdy leather tabs to help prevent tearing/pulling at the fabric under excessive weight or stress. Handles that are sewn directly onto the exterior may come loose if they aren't thick enough to support the bag's weight or if the thread used is too thin.

Q&A

FM: Define "timeless."
MN/KW: Armani; the Hermès scarf; the Birkin bag.

FM: Define "fashion forward."
MN/KW: An innovator who pushes the envelope and who everyone incessantly copies: Tom Ford comes to mind.

FM: Who is your favorite style icon?
MN/KW: In the more than twenty-five years that Elsa Schiaparelli dominated the industry (along with Coco Chanel), she revolutionized the way people thought about fashion and personal style. She was successful in turning fashion into an art.

Bag Compartment Checklist

Your computer bag should have the following accessible compartments:

- **Cell and PDA/Blackberry pockets** should be easy to reach, with secure closings so phones and PDAs do not fall out of open pockets and get lost at the bottom of a large bag.

- **Cord/Battery pockets** should be large enough to accommodate batteries and cords and keep them tucked away so they don't come unwound and obstruct other compartments.

- **Zippered pocketbook or wallet compartment** should be within easy reach (preferably near the top of the bag's opening) if you don't plan to carry a separate purse or handbag.

- **Business card compartment** should be an open pocket located near the top of the bag; it should be only 5 inches (13 cm) deep so that you can pull a business card out quickly. (How many times a day are you reaching into your bag to pull out a business card? Enough to want to avoid fishing around in the abyss of your bag to find one.)

How to Travel and Arrive in Style

by Pamela Fiori of *Town & Country* magazine

In May 1993, Pamela Fiori made publishing history when she became the first female editor-in-chief of Town & Country *magazine, the premier luxury lifestyle magazine in America. Fiori, recipient of the Chevalier de l'Ordre du Mérite, France's highest civic honor, revitalized* Town & Country *by expanding the boundaries of the magazine to include a greater variety of topics, voices, personalities, and columns. Fiori was also named 2004's "Fashion Oracle of the Year" by Saks Fifth Avenue.*

In the days of curbside porters and other personal service provided at an airport, the weight and size of your luggage was of less concern than it is today (and not just because of increased security). In a sprawling airport, you may be required to walk quite a distance or take airport transportation to your gate, and delays mean you will be spending more time waiting for your flight; everywhere you go your bag must go with you. And after all that, you have to lift your bag into the overhead compartment—so the best rule is to never take what you cannot handle alone.

LUGGAGE

Making your task easier is luggage on wheels, one of the greatest boons to modern travel, second only to ATMs abroad. Most airlines allow one piece of luggage, provided it will fit in the overhead bin, and one tote bag (into which I slip my handbag, a clutch).

CHOOSING LUGGAGE:

- **Size:** Most airlines specify a limitation of 45 linear inches (114 linear cm) (this means the height added to the length and depth) for carry-on luggage—this includes external expandable pockets. International carriers generally allow 62 linear inches (157 linear cm), and while airlines may accept larger bags, there is often a high fee.

- **Weight:** The airlines have a limitation of 40 pounds (18 kg), so the best bags are light, weighing 9 to 10 pounds (4.1–4.5 kg) empty. (That's one of the things you pay for in an expensive bag: a light but strong frame.)

- **Handle:** The bag should have a telescopic handle that retracts and extends easily with the click of a button.

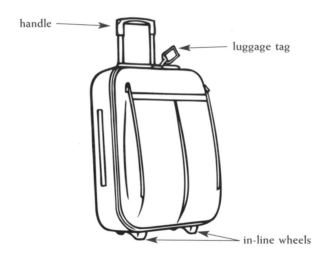

- **Wheels:** Look for durable in-line skate wheels that are not only smooth but quiet. Wheels situated near the outer edges of the case are best. It's a simple matter of geometry: The wheels have to be far enough apart to provide the base of the triangle formed when you extend the handle. If the wheels are too close together, the case will wobble when you pull it.

- **Material:** The biggest wear and tear for a carry-on comes from abrasion, and so the fabric must be durable (leather is nice, but it's quite heavy), like a Ballistic or Cordura nylon in a high denier. (The denier measures the fineness of the weave, so the higher the denier, the stronger the fabric.)
- **Hardware:** Zippers should not be too close to the edge, to prevent splitting. The suitcase should have tight double stitching and multiple rivets where there are handles.
- **Tags:** Always have luggage tags firmly attached to your baggage with your name, phone number, and business address (or home address if the flap or tag covers the information).

CHOOSING A TOTE BAG: The tote bag you carry must have a zipper so that when it goes through security nothing will spill out of it. The under-the-seat measurement for these bags is about 20 inches (51 cm), and I suggest a dark-colored canvas with a contrasting trim. Mine is black canvas with brown leather trim, made by T. Anthony, and I have had it for years.

ATTIRE

GENERAL STRATEGY: I know it's really uncomfortable up there at 30,000 feet (9,100 m) in cramped quarters with no leg room. But that doesn't mean you should wear your jammies or dress like you're ready to run the marathon. Solution: Wear comfortably fitted (not baggy or sloppy) tops and bottoms in solid colors, preferably navy blue, black, or gray. And, with all the new materials available in clothing, there is absolutely no excuse to look wrinkled (unless it's your skin, in which case you should see a dermatologist immediately). If it is a particularly long flight, it is even more important to dress comfortably as well as (not instead of) dressing stylishly because you will probably drink a lot of fluids to avoid dehydration. You'll also be confined to one place, nowhere near a gym, and at close quarters to your seatmate, who you may or may not know.

CHOOSING YOUR ATTIRE: I usually wear the following on every flight: a pair of black knit or microfiber slacks and a simple boatneck or crewneck knit top in the same color. Over that, I wear a lightweight jacket—same or similar fabric— and I carry a heavier jacket that I either keep with me or store in the overhead bin. Additionally, I take a lightweight cashmere scarf or shawl in a bright, pretty color. The cabin temperature fluctuates wildly, and I tend to feel the cold easily, so layering works well for me. You'll probably be asked to remove your shoes before going through security, so wear socks or stockings or put a pair of inexpensive flips flops in your carry-on.

For shoes, I like low-heeled loafers or a pair of ballerina flats. I might also wear a pair of low-heeled slides. Don't wear stilettos on board unless you want to risk a sprained ankle. Knee-length boots are much too constraining (if you take them off and then try putting them on again at the end of the flight, you may not succeed because your feet will inevitably have swelled).

Q&A

FM: Define "trendy."
PF: Ponchos—great if you don't mind looking like you live in an Andes mountain village.

FM: Define "timeless."
PF: A top-quality cashmere scarf or stole that is lightweight and colorful. I like coral, because it goes with everything and works all year round.

FM: Who is your favorite style icon?
PF: Jackie Kennedy Onassis. She had it all. She knew it. And she wore it like a glove.

What to Carry-On

What I Always Carry-On
- prescription medication (in my tote bag)
- moisturizer
- iPod
- cell phone and Blackberry (and their respective chargers)
- some jewelry (mostly earrings)
- a watch (two if I am changing time zones—I keep one on New York time and set the other to the time of my destination)
- a pair of cotton socks (in case your feet get cold—mine always do)
- small-sized hair conditioner (most hotels have shampoos, but don't always have conditioner)
- toothbrush, toothpaste, floss, and a minimal amount of makeup
- Jo Malone toilet water in Grapefruit or Lime, Basil, and Mandarin
- a pad and extra pens
- at least one paperback book
- several magazines (which I usually leave on the plane)

What I Never Take with Me
- anything made of linen
- anything with pleats or ruffles
- jewelry that has great sentimental or monetary value (which, if you lost it, would break your heart)
- heavy pieces of jewelry, like multistrand necklaces and bracelets
- a robe (because there's usually one at the hotel)
- hair dryer (ditto)
- big glass bottles of anything
- hardcover books

How to Get It Together for a Wedding

by Suzanne Williamson Pollak of Suzanne Pollak Designs Inc.

Suzanne Williamson Pollak has crossed the country lecturing on topics ranging from business etiquette to entertaining and wedding planning. The former interior design spokesperson for Federated Department Stores, Pollak (and her husband) researched and restored a 1780 Federal southern mansion in Beaufort, South Carolina, using eighteenth-century masonry techniques, reproduction lighting and landscaping, historical paint colors, and museum-quality Federal furniture. She is the author of Entertaining for Dummies *and coauthor of* The Pat Conroy Cookbook.

In today's more mobile life, weddings are no longer local affairs, and as such, you may be invited to several events over the course of a weekend for which you will need different kinds of clothes. The act of planning for a weekend's worth of festivities being held in another city throws most people into a panic. But it's not so tricky. When it comes to the actual wedding, the location does not dictate the dress—the time of day and type of ceremony do. As a result, the same outfit works for a formal evening wedding, whether it's in New York or Nashville.

For the rest of the festivities, there are no hard and fast rules, but here location does come into play. Are you staying in a ski resort, a beach club, or a big city hotel? Even when the invitations to the related events (like a wedding breakfast) don't give you an indication as to level of formality, one telephone call to someone who knows the bride/groom's family is all it takes to find out whether to expect a jewels-and-Bentley rehearsal dinner or a pig-picking barbecue. You can never go wrong with a middle-of-the road approach—anything to avoid being overdressed, undressed, or even outfitted in something too see-through, too tight, or too look-at-me! As any good guest knows, it's all about the bride.

STEP 1: Decode the invitation. Once you know the location of the wedding weekend, track the local weather, then list the number of events and the time of day each is occurring. You also need to plan for any down time (like hanging out by the pool or playing golf). The schedule of events and the weather report dictate your packing list.

STEP 2: Begin with the main event, and mix and match from there. Since you can't bring your entire closet (and you really can't), the other outfits you need should tie in with your ceremony/reception selection. It's like putting a puzzle together. Clear off your bed and lay out your ceremony/reception outfit along with every accessory that accompanies it, right down to earrings and underpinnings. Now lay out your related event outfits and stand back to look at the big picture. Where are your crossovers?

Can your beaded clutch and that fabulous brooch you intend to wear with your silk wrap shirt and long skirt to the wedding be paired with some cigarette pants and a cashmere top for the rehearsal dinner? If not, find something that can. Believe me, the effort that goes into planning a wardrobe of weekend festivities should take place in your home, not at the other end when you discover you've brought too much and still have nothing to wear.

STEP 3: Try tone-on-tone options. Dressing in tone-on-tone outfits (solids are more versatile than patterns) is another way to save space and still look good. Working with different shades of the same color for skirts and trousers—like lilac and plum, or bone and brown—is a good way to coordinate your wardrobe so that you can layer (darker colors hold up for a second wear better than light ones will). A pencil skirt can go with lightweight tees as well as a little cropped jacket or cocktail cardigan in the same color family, and there you have an informal, day casual, and slightly dressy night look tied into the same basic. You can even pop that little cropped jacket on over a pair of jeans for a super casual but still pulled together look.

STEP 4: Remember portability and comfort. And just in case you think it's all about the look—it's not. Clothes need to be foldable. If you love the look of a long skirt for evening, forget the ballroom style and pick something with a narrower silhouette—something that doesn't require you to purchase another seat on the plane.

And your clothing also needs to be comfortable (within reason): Weddings are long (most are $3\,1/2$ to 4 hours), and you will be standing up for much of that time. With that in mind, consider limiting yourself to three pairs of shoes: The ones you wear while traveling, the shoes you bring to accessorize your ceremony/reception outfit, and one other pair.

EXTRA HELP

A Wedding Cheat Sheet

- **Evening big city**: Black is appropriate
- **Evening winter**: Jacket and long satin skirt
- **Daytime winter**: Formal winter suit (in winter, heavier fabrics such as brocades and satins—but not too bulky to pack)
- **Afternoon**: Tea-length dress (anywhere from just under the knee to right above the ankle)
- **Resort**: Chiffon tops, silky long skirts, palazzo pants for rehearsal dinner
- **Casual country, outside**: Long and flowing, floral, lighter fabric such as chiffon, hats
- **Rehearsal dinner**: Dress or suit, dressy pants
- **Luncheon or brunch before wedding**: More casual, like pants with flowery top
- **Sunday breakfast**: Funkier, wear what you will travel in

---

STEP 5: Accessories are key. Accessories can make even the most basic outfit look totally individual. In addition to your jewelry, you always want to bring a great wrap and a small evening clutch. Nothing brings an outfit down like a daytime bag with a nighttime look.

The key accessories are your shoes, bag, and jewelry. Go a little wild no matter how conservative or old you are. A conservative black pant suit for a holiday wedding can stand the sparkle of silvery metallic shoes and envelope bag and a brooch with sparkly stones (faux or real).

Accessories are easy to pack. Bags, shoes, jewelry, and wraps take up very little space in a suitcase, but these pieces have the wow factor once they adorn you.

Q&A

FM: Define "trendy."
SWP: Any new "it" bag. What a shame about the bag—so much money, so "yesterday" so soon.

FM: Who is film's most fashionable leading man?
SWP: Steve McQueen, because he exuded confidence. And today, André 3000, because he doesn't copy anyone. He creates style. Style is confidence and confidence is style.

FM: Favorite fashion scene from a movie
SWP: The scene around the van der Luyden table in Martin Scorsese's period epic *The Age of Innocence*. From the elaborate dress, the dizzying amount of silverware, and the rhythm of the course-by-course dinner, it is scary, confusing, and absolutely wonderful.

How to Keep Your Look Fresh

by Linda Roberts of Private Edition

Linda Roberts is the owner of Private Edition, a Nashville retail store (and mail-order catalog) devoted to cutting-edge beauty brands. Roberts is also the founder and cocreator of Therapy Systems, skincare products rooted in pharmaceutical and botanical ingredients. Her latest retail venture, Cosmetic Market & Take-Out Café (also in Nashville), combines fun and functionality as it offers the convenience of the corner grocery to those shopping for prestige beauty products.

There comes a time in every woman's life—and it comes at different times to different women—when you realize that you must take more care with your hair, makeup, and wardrobe. However, many times an attempt to take more care tips over into becoming too careful, and the secret to keeping your look young and fresh means finding the middle point. While everyone's style is different, following these guidelines will help to keep your look modern and up-to-date.

STEP 1: Beware the matchy-matchy. When you are younger and can't really afford to buy everything you want, you tend to improvise in your wardrobe. As a result, your combinations are a little off-center—a little funkier—and that's great. As you get older, you tend to have all the right pieces, but that doesn't mean you should wear them all at one time. Mess it up a little bit. Keep experimenting.

STEP 2: Keep current with your curves. As your body changes, so should your clothing silhouette. As your natural waistline begins to thicken (and it happens to all of us), try flat-front skirts and slacks with side or back zippers—no pleats or slash pockets that will add bulk to places where you already have it. Skirts and slacks that have a bit of a dropped waist (instead of cinching you around the middle) are more flattering, and so is a top that cuts right across the stomach (instead of a longer length in an attempt to "hide" it). The result is a leaner look. This is especially true for jeans—an American classic no matter what your age. Get a pair that hits you about an inch (2.5 cm) below the belly button. However, once jeans drop more than two inches (5 cm) something else drops along with it—your stomach, right over the waistband!

STEP 3: Add the right accessories. You should have two basic core wardrobes: one in black and one in a neutral color. Then it is easy to add great accessories, like a wrap in a soft color to create a nice illusion near the face. Invest in one incredible bag and two pairs of shoes each season—and here you can take advantage of what is happening in fashion at the moment.

In jewelry, one large piece is more modern looking than several small "precious" pieces (vintage being the exception), and the same goes for a brightly colored oversized watch that can become a great signature accessory. Keep this in mind: Necklaces against clothing look old. Necklaces against skin look young.

STEP 4: Keep your legs bare. Whenever the weather permits, lose the panty hose and never wear socks or tights under a pant. It's sexier to see a bit of skin peeking out between the hem and the shoe. There may be a few exceptions to this rule, such as a black tie event during a blizzard—I cannot think of any more!

STEP 5: Be a nut about your hair! There is an old saying that the older you get, the shorter and lighter your hair should be, and it's true—up to a point. Don't go to extremes. Hair that is too light in color can wash you out totally, which is extremely aging. This definitely applies to highlighting. Avoid it by getting highlights and lowlights. Highlights brighten and lighten, whereas lowlights add depth and contrasting color to the hair. This will give you the overall softening effect you want as well as the natural highs and lows of color, adding movement and the appearance of texture to your hair. In the end, your complexion should "pop" and you won't need as much makeup.

As far as your haircut goes, disregard what is in style at the moment—what is in style is what looks good on you. But again, within reason: Beware the dreaded time warp. Unless you are trying to become an icon yourself, stretch a little. The only absolute is that your hair should have movement regardless of length, be it short, medium length, or long. This can mean a choppy bang or soft pieces around your face. What's aging is hair that is too short or too long. Keep it soft and moving, and, dear God, throw away that can of hairspray!

STEP 6: Minimize your makeup—less is definitely more. Go ahead and wear foundation if you want it to sink into every line on your face. A younger look can be achieved with a tinted moisturizer with a minimum SPF of 15. This gives you a fresher look while protecting the skin. It will definitely look more natural, like skin, not makeup. Brush on a loose mineral powder for a more polished look. A mineral powder contains no talc, which gives you a very soft finish while acting as a sun block without any chemicals or added ingredients. Give yourself a natural glow by applying a cream blush, as it is particularly good for dry skin and is very long-lasting. If you are traveling and don't have time to touch up before a special event, top off the cream blush with a little powder blush. It will be so long-lasting that you will have to wash it off.

Now to the eyes. Everyone, even blondes, should use black mascara. It is the most natural effect you can achieve. Notice that I did not say 12 coats of black mascara. If you want a natural look, put one coat on your upper lashes only. If you want a more dramatic look, apply several. Just spare us the clumps and globs!

So much for makeup. You can see how quick and easy it is to have a young natural look. This is all you need. Eyeliner and shadow are all nice touches, but they are just not a prerequisite for the grocery store. Add them when you have a few extra minutes or want to polish your look. Remember the most important point—use an extremely light touch.

Q&A

FM: Define "trendy."
LR: Anything that looks inappropriate on you.

FM: Define "timeless."
LR: A pair of well-cut jeans, a white blouse, and diamond studs.

FM: Define "fashion forward."
LR: No question about it—have the best accessories.

How to Tame Your Closet

by Brenda Kinsel of Inside Out, a Style and Wardrobe Consulting Company

Brenda Kinsel, the owner of Inside Out, a Style and Wardrobe Consulting Company, which is based in the San Francisco Bay area, has been matching people's clothes to their personalities, passions, and lifestyles since 1985. Featured on Oprah *and NPR, Kinsel is a fashion columnist for the* Pacific Sun *and the bestselling author of* 40 Over 40: 40 Things Every Woman Over 40 Needs to Know About Getting Dressed *and* In the Dressing Room with Brenda.

Most likely, you have been telling yourself for weeks, months, maybe even years, that you need to do something about your closet. When it takes you more than five minutes to get dressed in the morning, when you're wearing the same three outfits over and over but your closet is overflowing, or you reach for items but can't wear them—the hem is hanging down, there's a bleach stain on the front of your favorite shirt—you need to make peace with your wardrobe.

A closet edit is something you should do at least once a year, devoting a full day to the task just before you change over to the fall/winter or spring/summer season. By eliminating what doesn't work, you are free to wear everything in your closet, looking and feeling great every time you get dressed. You'll feel like you've lost ten pounds (4.5 kg)!

STEP 1: Gather your supplies beforehand. You'll need plenty of empty boxes or garden-sized trash bags, a full-length mirror, and a portable clothes rack (or in a pinch, set up an ironing board for more sorting space). Purchase hangers with a uniform design (see "Choosing Hangers," next page) to replace all those thin metal hangers from the drycleaners with more substantial versions. Pick up a good-looking storage box to store clothing that may not fit but has sentimental value.

Choosing Hangers

- Choose padded hangers to help delicate garments (like lightweight knits, silks, and evening wear) retain their shoulder shape.

- Choose curved wooden hangers for heavier garments like suit jackets, blazers, and coats. (Hang the garment with the curved side facing out.)

- Make sure that the movable clips on wooden skirt and pants hangers are rubber lined to prevent crimp marks on the fabric of the waistbands. Hang flat-front pants from the outermost edges of the waistband (without stretching the fabric). Pants with iron-in creases should be folded along that crease and clipped at the corners of the waistband.

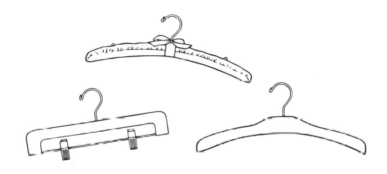

STEP 2: Empty out and clean your closet. Hang clothes on the portable clothes rack, place them on your bed, or drape them on the ironing board. Clean the closet shelves, sweep or vacuum the floor, and dust down the walls. Hang sachets of lavender on a handful of hangers to give your clothes a fresh smell (it will also help fight bugs).

STEP 3: Try on everything and begin the sorting process. If an item fits or flatters, put it on a new hanger. If a garment needs repair, set it aside in a "To Do" pile. (Plan to have all repairs completed in three weeks.)

STEP 4: Arrange the clothes in your closet by color, from light to dark, so they look as orderly as a fresh box of Crayola waxed colors. Blouses, pants, skirts, and dresses all hang together if they are the same color. If you have large groups of one color, arrange the items from short to long: blouses first, then jackets, skirts, and pants. Dressy things will hang with casual things to inspire fabulous combinations you wouldn't have considered.

Note: Some items of clothing, such as cotton sweaters, silk turtlenecks, or lightweight cashmere sweaters are perfect for the transitional time between seasons. Retire these pieces from your closet only when you are truly in the thick of the season, from summer to fall or winter to spring. It is normal to have an overlap of pieces like these within a fashion season.

STEP 5: Sort the clothes that didn't make the cut. Put clothes that are stained, ripped, and not repairable in the trash. The clothes that don't fit or just aren't "you" anymore may be right for someone else. Place them in a box to go to a consignment store or favorite charity. If you absolutely must hang onto some favorites you think you'll wear someday when you have lost some weight or when circumstances call for them, place them in your souvenir box, to be stored in an extra closet with your photos and other keepsakes. Your current closet should hold only your current working wardrobe.

STEP 6: Make a chart of all the outfits in your newly organized closet. You may now have fresh ideas about wearing new combinations of outfits. Write out the new combos and keep the list in your closet for reference. As you create more outfits during the year, keep recording them, and you will always have something wonderful to wear. It will also be easy to see if you are repeatedly buying tops without the right bottoms or always buying pants but never having an array of tops to choose from.

⚠ **"It's not that I love it; it's just that it was so expensive."** Here are three options for those pieces that you can't/won't wear or that aren't appropriate to your body shape, coloring, personal style, or lifestyle.

1. Gift your mistakes to friends or relatives who are more suited to them. The sooner you gift them, the longer the giftee has to enjoy them.

2. Help someone else get on her feet. There are many worthwhile organizations that will take clothing and give it to women who are getting back into the workforce and can't afford that interview outfit or the first week of outfits for a new job. (One such organization is Career Closets.) You can also find local organizations that help AIDS patients, battered women, or those in recovery for drugs or alcohol addiction.

3. Take your current rejects to a consignment store. You will usually receive half of what they charge their customers for the garments they sell. Again, recognize your mistakes early so your clothes will be appealing to shoppers.

FM: What's the worst fashion faux pas?

BK: Settling for clothes that kind of, sort of, work, but don't really.

FM: Who is your favorite style icon?

BK: Jacqueline Kennedy Onassis: She never apologized for boldly loving fashion.

FM: What's your favorite fashion scene from a movie?

BK: In the remake of *Ocean's Eleven*, when George Clooney exits prison to find Brad Pitt waiting for him, outfitted in a seventies-style leisure suit and spread-collar shirt, Clooney says, "Ted Nugent called. He wants his shirt back."

How to Organize Your Shoes

by Susan Zises Green of Susan Zises Green Inc.

Susan Zises Green, whose creative mix of traditional European and American designs has gained a following from Manhattan to Palm Beach, is a seven-time participant in the Kips Bay Boys and Girls Club Decorators Showhouse, a yearly event highlighting the work of the country's most prestigious interior designers. She has lectured on design in the New York Times/Architectural Digest Home Design Showhouse, The Doyle Gallery, The International Majolica Society, *and various other venues. Her work has appeared in* Architectural Digest *and* House Beautiful, *where she was selected as one of the "Top 125 Designers in America" for the past three years.*

Many women "forget" certain shoes simply because their closets are not organized properly. But storing shoes so that you know what you have must be part of your entire closet scheme. If you are willing to commit to a "place for everything and everything in its place," you can have full access to your shoes without the high cost of a customized closet.

I store my shoes in drawers that fully extend, grouped as I group my clothing: according to color, not style, occasion, or material. I also label the drawers by color so that when my clothing calls for brown shoes (or something in that color family), I open the corresponding drawer to see all my choices. Forget the hanging shoe holders and door racks, or individual shoe bags with tiny labels that I can't read without my glasses. My technique works and is easy to replicate within any price range.

STEP 1: View your closet as a whole, rethinking what needs to be stored there. Most of our homes have untapped storage space, and you should consider all the possibilities to house off-season clothing (or anything else that is not crucial to your wardrobe) somewhere other than your closet—even under the beds.

STEP 2: Determine the best place to store your shoes so you can get to them. Newsflash: When it comes to storing your shoes, visibility is not as critical as location. In most closets, horizontal space is limited, so this typically means vertical storage. Depending upon the configuration of your closet, you can either work from the top down (utilizing the space above your clothing) or the floor up (which I prefer).

STEP 3: Measure the amount of space you have to devote to shoe storage. This helps you to determine the maximum-size shoeboxes or drawers you can use.

STEP 4: Research your storage container options. The storage area of any super store will present you with many choices, from a lightweight, rolling chest of drawers with stackable components for adaptable height (just make sure the drawers extend fully) to stackable recycled fiberboard (for durability and strength) with a laminated finish that resists moisture. My choice is drawers that are 23 inches (58 cm) wide by 21 inches (53 cm) deep, and that hold 12 to 15 pairs of heels in each. Any way you do it, uniformity is important for practical and aesthetic reasons. Your closet should be yet another place in your home to display your favorite items—not a way to hide a mess.

STEP 5: Before you buy, experiment. Use something with the approximate measurements of the containers you have selected (even a cardboard box) and see how they will fit or stack.

STEP 6: Sort your shoes by color—not style, occasion, or material. I know it will be strange at first, but you'll learn to love this storage solution, not only for its efficiency but because it allows you easy access to all the shoes that work within the color family. This may even give you some combinations you never thought of wearing. One exception: Since your sports and outdoor activity shoes are bought by function and rarely color, store them together so your gardening clogs won't scuff your ballet flats.

STEP 7: Interlock your shoes heel to toe to fit as many as possible in the drawers. Very high heels should lay on their sides, interlocked, unless you build taller drawers to accomodate them. Long boots should be stored lying down, heel to toe, to prevent bending and creasing.

STEP 8: Label the drawers or boxes clearly and uniformly so the stack looks tidy when you open the closet door. Now when your outfit calls for black shoes, you'll see everything that works and never forget a pair of shoes that might be just what you need.

Q&A

FM. What's the best style tip you ever got, and from whom?
SZG: My mother told me to wear great shoes and a great bag, and to buy one dazzling outfit instead of three mediocre ones. She also told me that the best tailoring never goes out of style.

FM: What's the worst fashion faux pas?
SZG: Wearing too many labels at once.

FM: What's your favorite fashion scene from a movie?
SZG: The scene in *Gone with the Wind* when Scarlett tears down the green velvet curtains and fashions a dress out of them. It is a perfect example of how necessity is the mother of invention, and it combines my two favorite things: fashion and interior design.

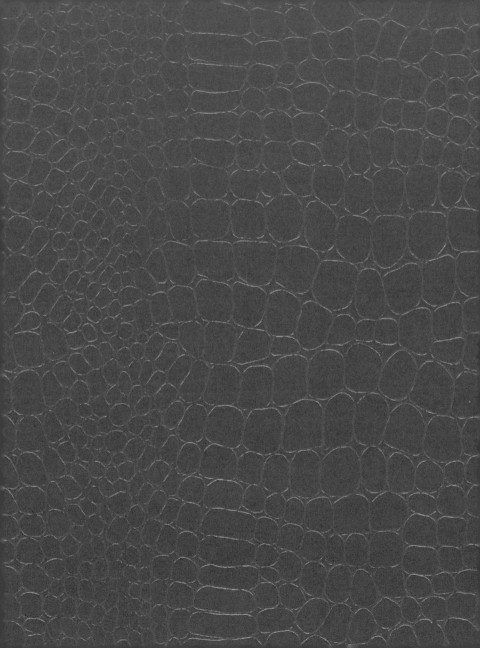

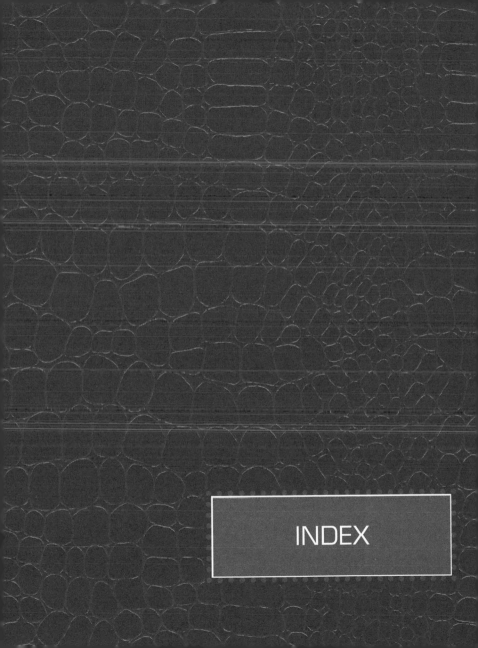

INDEX

Note: Page numbers in bold refer to illustrations.

ABOUT THE AUTHORS

FRANCINE MAROUKIAN, the author of *Town & Country's Elegant Entertaining*, *Esquire Eats*, and *Chef's Secrets* (Quirk Books, 2004), is a contributor to many magazines.

SARAH WOODRUFF works and lives in Glen Ridge, New Jersey, with her husband and their three children.

ACKNOWLEDGMENTS

The authors are grateful to Laura Blake Peterson, Nathan Bransford, and the support staff at Curtis Brown, as well as all the experts and their representatives who contributed time, energy, and stylish ideas to this book.

In addition, Francine Maroukian sends thanks to Patty Spaniak, Mitch Gruner, Joe Austin, and John Reitano for his timely how-to advice. Sarah Woodruff would like to thank her husband, Jay, and the many people who have shared, through advice and example, their ideas of elegance and grace.